40d

The Defendant's Rights Under English Law

The Defendant's Rights
Under English Law

DAVID FELLMAN, 1908 –

THE UNIVERSITY OF WISCONSIN PRESS

Madison, Milwaukee, and London   *1966*

Published by
The University of Wisconsin Press
Madison, Milwaukee, and London
P.O. Box 1379
Madison, Wisconsin 53701

Printed in the United States of America by
Vail-Ballou Press, Inc., Binghamton, New York

Library of Congress Catalog
Card Number 66-11803

41,566

For Norton and Mona

Preface

Since English legal categories in the public law field are quite unlike the American categories, perhaps a word of explanation should be given as to the focus of this book. American writers discuss the rights of defendants in criminal cases as a branch of constitutional law, although this subject is also considered under the heading of criminal law. In Britain, in the absence of written constitutional guarantees, supported by judicial review, what Americans call the constitutional rights of defendants in criminal cases are generally regarded as being merely part of the corpus of criminal law. Even so, English writers of texts on constitutional law do discuss in the criminal law field some of the rights of the individual, especially with respect to principles of personal liberty, such as the right to the writ of habeas corpus or freedom from general search warrants. I think I have touched on all of the rights of criminal law defendants which English writers customarily discuss under the heading of constitutional law, but I have gone far beyond that to include rules of law that relate to many more subjects. What I actually did was to start with a list of what American law writers consider the constitutional rights of the defendant, and then sought for their English analogues, however they may be classified in Britain. For example, the right of trial by jury, with all that that has come to mean, is a constitutional right in the United States. In Britain it is subsumed under the heading of criminal law. Thus I have lifted this right out of its natural place in English law and shifted it over to join all other rights which we in the United States regard as being constitutional in nature.

In short, when a person in the United States is accused of a crime, our state and federal constitutional law gives him the protection of a considerable body of legal rights. In this essay I seek to explore the prevailing English rules of law on roughly the same subjects. Thus it is not material, for the purposes of this essay, that the defendant's right to a public trial is guaranteed by constitutional provisions in the United States and by statutes in Britain. Even in a formal sense it is probably not true that our constitutional right to a public trial is any more solidly secured than the English statutory right, since Parliament is no more likely to abandon this highly-regarded right by the enactment of a repealing statute than are the people of the United States through the seemingly more complex and difficult process of constitutional amendment. The appeal of an Englishman accused of crime to the rights of fair trial is not really very different from the appeal of an American defendant.

The special difficulty of this study is that it does not follow established English categories of legal classification. It must therefore be stressed that this essay does not even pretend to be a survey of English criminal law, much less one of English criminology. Since most American rights in this area are procedural in character, this essay is largely concerned with certain procedural elements of English criminal law.

Thus my purpose here is a very modest one: to describe those rules of law which we in the United States have come to regard as the constitutional rights of persons accused of crime. By rules of law I mean simply statutes of Parliament, as construed authoritatively by the courts, and that body of law which the judges themselves have made in the course of rendering decision in concrete cases. Since English law is very ancient, and the statutes and judicial precedents very numerous, I have tried to limit the citation of statutes and cases to those which control decisions today.

This leaves out a great deal. I have not been concerned with the sociology of crime, or with the politics of criminal law enforcement, or with problems of penology. Nor have I been concerned with the great body of substantive English criminal law. These are, of course, interesting and important subjects, and there is a vast literature on them, but it was not my intention to write about them.

One final caveat. I did not intend to write an essay in comparative law. In order to give some intelligible form (for an American reader) to a body of legal principles relating to English defendants in criminal cases, I have borrowed familiar American law categories, even though they do not fit into current English legal systems of classification and analysis. But I have made no systematic effort to compare American with English law and practice in describing the rights of those who in England are accused of a crime. In the text I call attention to some similarities and differences between the two legal systems, and in the footnotes I have given citations to a few controlling United States Supreme Court decisions that suggest points of contrast or similarity. But a thorough analysis of American law would have resulted in a far more ambitious essay than I ever intended to write at this time. In sum, my purpose is to describe, with suitable documentation of authority, the legal content of the rights of an Englishman who is caught in the toils of the criminal law. In the final chapter I try to point up some of the most arresting features of this body of law, as they appear to an American student of the subject.

I suppose I cast a small net; but then, this is a small book.

I desire to express my appreciation to several members of the faculty of the London School of Economics and Political Science, from whom I learned much in conversation about the English governmental system: Professor William A. Robson, now Emeritus, Professor Richard Pear, now at Nottingham University, and Mr. Leslie Wolf-Phillips, Lecturer in Political Science. Of course they have no responsibility for anything I have written in this book, and have never seen the manuscript. I should also like to express my appreciation to the Trustees of the William F. Vilas Trust for their financial assistance. I am deeply indebted to the staff of the University of Wisconsin Press for excellent editorial work, and in particular I take this opportunity to express my thanks to Mrs. Isobel A. Korbel, who wields a very sharp pencil indeed.

DAVID FELLMAN

Madison, Wisconsin
June 1, 1965

Contents

Preface   *vii*

I   *The English System of Criminal Courts*   3

II   *The Preliminaries*   *14*

Arrest, 14; Bail, 20; Prosecution, 28

III   *The Police and the Accused*   *34*

Police Interrogation, 34; Confessions, 45; Searches and Seizures, 52; Use of Wrongfully Secured Evidence, 59; Habeas Corpus, 61

IV   *The Right to a Fair Trial*   67

Some Elements of a Fair Trial, 67; Public Trial, 71; The Concept of Natural Justice, 75; Right to Counsel, 80; Double Jeopardy, 88

V   *Conduct of the Trial*   *97*

The Jury, 97; The Burden of Proof, 103; Comment by the Judge, 111

VI   *An Evaluation*   *116*

Index   *133*

The Defendant's Rights Under English Law

I

The English System
of Criminal Courts

IN AN ultimate sense, the Englishman's claim to justice in the administration of the criminal law rests on the existence of the rule of law.[1] It was recently pointed out by an English scholar that "everyone, high or low, must be prepared to justify his acts by a reference to some statutory or common law power which authorises him to act precisely in the way in which he claims he can act. Superior orders or state necessity are no defence to an action otherwise illegal."[2] This notion is re-enforced by the general rule that statutes are con-

1. This book is concerned only with the courts of England and Wales and not with all the courts of Great Britain as a whole. Scottish courts and law are quite distinctive.
2. R. F. V. Heuston, *Essays in Constitutional Law* (London: Stevens, 1961), pp. 38–39. See 7 Halsbury's *Laws of England*, 3rd ed., pp. 195–96: "The so-called liberties of the subject are really implications drawn from the two principles that the subject may say or do what he pleases, provided he does not transgress the substantive law, or infringe the legal rights of others, whereas public authorities (including the Crown) may do nothing but what they are authorised to do by some rule of common law or statute. Where public authorities are not authorised to interfere with the subject, he has liberties. . . . Further, since Parliament is sovereign, the subject cannot possess guaranteed rights such as are guaranteed to the citizen by many foreign constitutions. It is well understood that certain liberties are highly

3

strued in favor of protecting private rights. "It is clear," Lord Blackburn once wrote, "that the burden is on those who seek to establish that the legislature intended to take away the private rights of individuals to show that by express words or by necessary implication such an intention appears." [3]

As in the United States, English law touching on the rights of one who has been accused of crime rests on a recognition of the basic inequality of the parties involved. "The discovery and punishment of crime," Lord MacDermott, Lord Chief Justice of Northern Ireland, pointed out in his notable Hamlyn Lectures, "are functions which produce a dramatic preponderance of power on the part of the State. Against the wealth and resources of the prosecution the accused stands relatively poor and alone and, far more often than not, his case and its personal problems arouse little general interest or concern." [4] Such elements of English law as the high development of the action of trespass, the availability of such prerogative orders as the writ of habeas corpus, and trial by jury, "by unprofessional representatives of public opinion," [5] all point in the direction of helping the weaker party. Similarly, it is a basic principle of English law that criminal offenses should be defined with certainty and precision, that everyone enjoys the presumption of innocence, and that

prized by the people, and that in consequence Parliament is unlikely, except in emergencies, to pass legislation constituting a serious interference with them." See also Sir W. Ivor Jennings, *The Law and the Constitution* (5th ed.; London: University of London Press, 1959), Chap. 8.

3. Metropolitan Asylum District v. Hill (1881) 6 App. Cas. 193, 208 (H.L.).

4. Lord MacDermott, *Protection from Power under English Law* (London: Stevens, 1957), p. 13.

5. Halsbury's *Laws of England*, 3rd ed., p. 196.

the burden of proof to establish guilt beyond a reasonable doubt is on the prosecution.

For the most part, these principles are applied by courts which specialize in criminal law work.[6] At the base of the system are the magistrates' courts, which handle about 97 per cent of all the criminal cases in England and Wales.[7] In the larger cities there are salaried, fully qualified stipendiary magistrates, but in most of the country the justices are public-spirited laymen who are appointed by the Lord Chancellor on the recommendation of the Lord Lieutenant of the county or, in some boroughs, of local advisory committees and who serve without pay.[8] They know little about the law and rely heavily on their clerks. The justices of the peace, as judicial officers, date from the days of Edward III in the middle of the fourteenth century,[9] and now number about 25,000, serving over a thousand magis-

6. The best treatise on English courts is R. M. Jackson, *The Machinery of Justice in England* (3rd ed.; Cambridge: Cambridge University Press, 1960). See also Pendleton Howard, *Criminal Justice in England* (New York: Macmillan, 1931); R. C. K. Ensor, *Courts and Judges in France, Germany and England* (Oxford: Oxford University Press, 1933); H. G. Hanbury, *English Courts of Law* (2nd ed.; Oxford: Oxford University Press, 1953); J. D. Devlin, *Criminal Courts and Procedure* (London: Butterworth, 1960); Peter Archer, *The Queen's Courts* (London: Penguin Books, 1956).

7. G. H. Hatherill, "Criminal Law Enforcement in England," 31 U. of Kan. City L. Rev. 102, 130 (1963).

8. Some persons are justices ex officio, e.g., the chairmen of urban and rural district councils, and some borough mayors. On the origin of the advisory committees, see J. M. Lee, "Parliament and the Appointment of Magistrates," 13 Parl. Affairs 85 (1959–60). See also Sir George Phillips Coldstream, "Judicial Appointments in England," 43 J. Am. Jud. Soc. 41 (1959).

9. 18 Edw. 3, stat. 2, c. 2 (1344). The title "justice of the peace" was created by the Justices of the Peace Act, 1360. See C. A. Beard, *The Office of Justice of the Peace in England* (New York: Columbia University Press, 1904), reprinted by Burt Franklin (New York, 1962).

trates' courts. They deal with summary offenses [10] and the less serious indictable offenses and also serve as examining magistrates in respect to indictable offenses.[11] While a single magistrate may issue a summons or discharge the functions of an examining justice, a magistrates' court must include at least two justices when conducting trials.[12] With several exceptions, generally speaking the magistrates are limited to imposing up to six months' imprisonment as punishment.[13]

The next higher criminal courts are the Courts of Quarter Sessions, of which there are about two hundred and fifty in England and Wales. In the counties, these courts are conducted by no fewer than two and no more than nine justices. Under the terms of a recent statute [14] the chairman of Quarter Sessions for any county must be a legally qualified lawyer, though he may or may not be salaried. In the boroughs, a Quarter Sessions court is presided over by a single salaried lifetime judge known as a Recorder. The Quarter Sessions courts have the power to try, with juries, all but the most serious indictable offenses.

The most serious offenses (e.g., murder, rape, robbery, treason) are tried in the Courts of Assize, for which there are seven circuits in England and Wales. These courts sit quarterly in designated Assize towns and are presided over by itinerant judges of the Queen's

10. For a graphic description of summary justice in the magistrates' courts, see Sybille Bedford, *The Faces of Justice* (London: Collins, 1961), Chap. 2. See also Archer, *The Queen's Courts,* Chap. 21, "Protecting the Innocent."

11. Magistrates' Courts Act, 1952, ss. 2 (3), 4–12, 18.

12. *Ibid.,* s. 98 (1).

13. Magistrates' courts also sit as juvenile courts (usually with three justices). The county or county borough councils also appoint lawyers or medical men to preside over coroners' courts.

14. Criminal Justice Administration Act, 1962, s. 5.

Bench Division. Thus they are in fact branches of the High Court of Justice.[15] The Assize courts have both civil and criminal jurisdiction, though they are mainly concerned with criminal cases, which are always given priority. The Assize courts have no appellate jurisdiction.

The governmental system of the Metropolitan London area was recently reorganized on a very large scale, and as a result its local courts are now in a state of flux. The reorganized court system was provided for in the Administration of Justice Act, 1964. Prior to the adoption of this act, however, there were in the London area thirteen Metropolitan magistrates' courts with twenty-nine magistrates, including a chief magistrate. Section 10 (1) of the 1964 act authorizes the appointment of as many as forty stipendiary magistrates in Metropolitan London. In addition, before the act there were lay justices' courts sitting in eight petty sessional divisions. There are today about three hundred justices on the active list of the County of London. These Petty Sessions courts grant liquor and betting licenses and have jurisdiction over offenses arising under about one hundred enactments. Their jurisdiction is partly concurrent with the Metropolitan magistrates' courts and partly exclusive. In 1962 an interdepartmental committee recommended the integration of these courts.[16] The Assize court for what is now called Greater London is the Central Criminal Court (Old Bailey), and it sits at

15. Supreme Court of Judicature (Consolidation) Act, 1925, s. 70. In 1960 the Queen's Bench Division was composed of the Lord Chief Justice and twenty-seven judges. Lord Goddard, "Organization and Jurisdiction of the Courts of England," 44 J. Am. Jud. Soc. 60–65 (1960).

16. Report of the Interdepartmental Committee on Magistrates' Courts in London, 1962, Cmd. 1606.

least four times a year.[17] Created in 1834, it is wholly
a trial court, with no appellate jurisdiction. At the present time this court sits in seven divisions: one is assigned
to a visiting judge of the Queen's Bench Division, one
to the Recorder of the City of London, one to the Common Serjeant of the City of London, and one to the
judge of the City of London Court sitting as a commissioner; the remaining three are presided over by additional commissioners. The Crown Courts Act, 1956,
created for Liverpool and Manchester central criminal
courts which are comparable to the Old Bailey.

A person who has been convicted in a magistrates'
court may appeal to Quarter Sessions in respect to any
question of law or fact or in respect to the sentence.
On appeal, the whole case is retried, Quarter Sessions
not being limited to the evidence given in the magistrates' court.[18] Quarter Sessions may affirm or reverse,
or may reduce or increase the punishment. On a point
of law the Quarter Sessions court may state a case for
the opinion of the High Court. If the matter does not
involve a conviction, Quarter Sessions, at its discretion,
may or may not state a case.[19] Where the matter involves a conviction, either party may ask the Court of
Quarter Sessions to have a case stated for the opinion
of the High Court on the purely legal issues of whether
the decision was wrong in the law or whether the proceedings were in excess of jurisdiction.[20] Justices may
refuse to state a case if they think the request is frivo-

17. Administration of Justice Act, 1964, s. 1 (1).
18. R. v. Hall, [1891] 1 Q.B. 747.
19. In this situation the High Court cannot compel Quarter Sessions,
by mandamus, to state a case. R. v. Somerset Justices, [1950] 1 K.B.
519.
20. Criminal Justice Act, 1925, s. 20. The prosecutor may ask the
justices to state a case where the information was dismissed. Reese v.
Read, [1949] 1 K.B. 377.

lous,[21] but the High Court has the power to issue mandamus to require a case to be stated.[22] The appeal is usually heard by a divisional court of the Queen's Bench Division consisting of three judges. The divisional court has the power to reverse, affirm, or amend, but it may not reduce the penalty.[23] In addition, appeal to Quarter Sessions may be abandoned by taking an appeal directly from a magistrates' court to the High Court, on a point of law.

The most important appeals court, for all serious offenses tried in the Assize or Quarter Sessions courts, or in the Central Criminal Court or the two Crown courts, is the Court of Criminal Appeal, which was created by the Criminal Appeal Act, 1907.[24] Usually, the Lord Chief Justice presides, and he sits with two other judges of the Queen's Bench Division, who are assigned to this court on a rotation basis. Appeal may be taken to the Court of Criminal Appeal on any question of law, as a matter of right. To bring up a question of fact, or a mixed question of fact and law, the leave of the court or the certificate of the trial judge must first be secured. Appeal against sentence is by leave of the court.[25] The "case-stated" procedure has always been available to the Court of Criminal Appeal,[26] but it has

21. Magistrates' Courts Act, 1952, s. 87 (5).

22. R. v. Derby Justices, *Ex parte* Waring, [1962] Crim. L. R. 392 (Q.B.D.) See D. M. Davies, "Magistrates' Courts: Appeal and Case Stated," [1962] Crim. L. Rev. 734–44.

23. Evans v. Hemingway (1887) 52 J.P. 134 (Q.B.D.).

24. See Delmar Karlen, *Appellate Courts in the United States and England* (New York: New York University Press, 1963), Chap. 7; Lord Goddard, "The Working of the Court of Criminal Appeal," 2 J. Soc. Pub. Teach. Law 1 (1952).

25. Leaves to appeal against conviction are granted to only about four per cent of the applicants. Goddard, "The Working of the Court of Criminal Appeal," p. 61.

26. Criminal Appeal Act, 1907, s. 20 (4).

been used very rarely.[27] At its discretion, the court may hear evidence itself, if, as the statute says, "they think it necessary or expedient in the interest of justice." [28] In a recent case [29] the Lord Chief Justice reviewed the reasons that guide the Court of Criminal Appeal in taking evidence. The court will take evidence which was not available at the trial; the evidence must be relevant to the issues; the evidence must be credible, i.e., "well capable of belief"; and it must be demonstrated that there might have been a reasonable doubt in the minds of the jury as to the defendant's guilt if the evidence had been given at the trial. Actually, the Court of Criminal Appeal hears fresh evidence only in the most exceptional circumstances, and the additional evidence must be such that it probably would have affected the verdict.[30] The court is not required to set aside a conviction merely because, on review, it concludes that there had been legal errors in the trial. The important proviso to the Criminal Appeal Act, 1907, section 4 (1), states that "the court may, notwithstanding that they are of opinion that the point raised in the appeal might be decided in favour of the appellant, dismiss the appeal if they consider that no substantial miscarriage of justice has actually occurred." [31]

The Court of Criminal Appeal has always had the

27. See D. A. Thomas, "Case Stated in the Court of Criminal Appeal," [1962] Crim. L. Rev. 820–27.

28. Criminal Appeal Act, 1907, s. 9.

29. R. v. Parks (1961) 46 Cr. App. R. 29, [1961] 1 W.L.R. 1484, [1961] 3 All E.R. 633 (C.C.A.). See G. D. Nokes, "Fresh Evidence in Criminal Appeals," [1963] Crim. L. Rev. 669–74.

30. R. v. Jordan (1956) 40 Cr. App. R. 152 (C.C.A); R. v. Harding (1936) 25 Cr. App. R. 190 (C.C.A.).

31. The court often refuses to regard legal errors as conclusive. For recent examples see R. v. McVitie (1960) 44 Cr. App. R. 201 (C.C.A.); R. v. Jones (1961) 46 Cr. App. R. 68 (C.C.A.). The House of Lords has ruled that this proviso cannot be applied in the case of

power to affirm or set aside the conviction appealed from, or to reduce or increase the sentence,[32] but prior to 1964 it had no power to order a new trial. Although it asked for this power as early as 1908 [33] and repeatedly thereafter,[34] there was strong resistance to giving this authority, apparently in large part because of the doctrine of double jeopardy.[35] A special departmental committee, reporting in 1954,[36] listed a number of additional reasons for not allowing the Court of Criminal Appeal to order new trials. There is always the danger that the second jury may have read about the case, and there was the fear that the second jury would infer that the Court of Criminal Appeal would not have directed a new trial unless it had considered the accused probably guilty. It was argued that it was unfair to put the accused through the ordeal and expense of a second trial because of some mistake on the part of the judge, the jury, or the prosecution. It was also argued that the mere existence of the power might tend to make the trial judge, the jury, or the prosecutor less careful at the trial, knowing that any defect would probably only result in a new trial. It was feared that the authority to

misdirection unless the court is satisfied that a reasonable jury properly directed would have reached the same conclusion. D.P.P. v. Stirland, [1944] A.C. 315 (H.L.).

32. Increase in sentence is extremely rare; there were only six such cases in 1963. *Report of the Interdepartmental Committee on the Court of Criminal Appeal* (Donovan Report), Cmd. 2755, August, 1965, p. 44.

33. R. v. Dyson, [1908] 2 K.B. 454, 458.

34. R. v. Stoddart (1909) 2 Cr. App. R. 217, 245 (C.C.A.); R. v. Ellison (1911) 7 Cr. App. R. 4 (C.C.A.). In R. v. Kingston (1948) 32 Cr. App. R. 183, 190 (C.C.A.), the court noted that it had asked for the power to order a new trial "time out of number."

35. Sir Patrick Devlin, *Trial by Jury* (London: Stevens, 1956), pp. 75–78.

36. Report of the Departmental Committee on New Trials in Criminal Cases, 1954, Cmd. 9150.

order new trials might make the Court of Criminal Appeal unduly insistent on technicalities, and that the spectacle of new trials would tend to lower public respect for the administration of justice. It was also noted that prolongation of criminal proceedings is against the public interest, since the administration of justice should be swift and final.

On the other hand, there were two main arguments in favor of permitting the appeal court to order new trials. First, without this power the court has no choice but to quash a conviction because of a serious irregularity or misdirection, and to enter a verdict of acquittal in the case of a dangerous criminal who was in fact guilty of a crime of violence. Second, it was argued that this power would diminish the number of cases where the Home Secretary must make extrajudicial inquiries, especially where fresh evidence was alleged to have come to light. The special committee concluded that, with certain safeguards, the Court of Criminal Appeal should have the power to order new trials in cases of fresh evidence.

With the enactment of the Criminal Appeal Act, 1964, the Court of Criminal Appeal was at long last given the power to order a new trial.[37] Section 1 of the statute provides that in cases tried on indictment, when an appeal against conviction is allowed by the Court of Criminal Appeal only by reason of the availability of fresh evidence, if "it appears to the Court that the interests of justice so required," instead of entering a verdict of acquittal it may order the appellant to be retried.[38] The appellant may be retried only for the

37. See G. D. Nokes, "The Criminal Appeal Act, 1964," [1964] Crim. L. Rev. 565–72.

38. The same power was given to the Courts-Martial Appeal Court, s. 4 and Sched. 2. This court is also made up of judges of Queen's Bench.

offense in respect to which his appeal was allowed, or in respect to any offense of which he could have been convicted at the original trial, or any offense charged in an alternative count on which no verdict had been given. If the accused is convicted on the retrial, the sentence may not be more severe than that originally imposed.

From the divisional court and the Court of Criminal Appeal, a final appeal proceeds to the House of Lords. Prior to 1960 no such appeal was possible unless the Attorney-General certified that a point of law of exceptional public importance was involved and that the appeal was desirable in the public interest.[39] Such appeals were in actual fact rarely allowed. During the period from 1907 to October 1960, only twenty-three successful applications for criminal appeals were made to the House of Lords, six at the instance of the prosecution and seventeen at the instance of the defense, and only eight appeals were ultimately allowed.[40] Under the Administration of Justice Act, 1960, a criminal appeal lies to the House of Lords, at the instance of either side, either from the divisional court of Queen's Bench or the Court of Criminal Appeal, on leave granted by either of these courts or by the House of Lords, provided that "a point of law of general public importance is involved in the decision . . . ."[41] There is reason to believe that in the future, as a consequence of the 1960 legislation, more criminal appeals will be taken to the House of Lords.

39. Criminal Appeal Act, 1907, s. 1 (6). See "Appeals to the House of Lords," [1957] Crim. L. Rev. 566–76.

40. D. G. T. Williams, "The Administration of Justice Act, 1960," [1961] Crim. L. Rev. 87–104. See Karlen, *Appellate Courts*, Chap. 8.

41. Administration of Justice Act, 1960, s. 1 (2). A refusal by a lower court of leave to appeal to the House of Lords is not appealable. Gelberg v. Miller, [1961] 1 W.L.R. 459 (H.L.) (E.).

II

The Preliminaries

Arrest

THAT the English view on the law of arrest is fastidious is reflected in a recent decision of the High Court of Justice, which held that the immigration authorities had exceeded their statutory powers in restraining an alien in transit and awarded £150 damages, since, as Barry, J., said, there had been an invasion of "the very precious right of liberty."[1] Similarly, the Royal Commission on the Police declared in 1960: "In a country jealous for the liberty of the subject, powers of arrest are not to be lightly conferred or wantonly exercised; and the constable must be vigilant both to use his authority adequately and instantly as occasion demands, and at the same time never to exceed it."[2] It was in this vein that Lord Denning had occasion to write in a 1959 opinion that "No one in this country

1. Kuchenmeister v. Home Office, [1958] 1 Q.B. 496, 513.
2. Royal Commission on the Police, *Interim Report*, 1960, Cmd. 1222, p. 12. See Davies v. Lisle, [1936] 2 K.B. 434, [1936] 2 All E.R. 213.

14

can be detained against his will except under the warrant of lawful authority; and when that warrant is required by law to be in writing, it must be produced on demand to the person detained and to any other person properly concerned to challenge the detention. When the legality of the detention has to be proved in a court of law the document itself must be produced. It is the best evidence and nothing else will do." [3] Speaking for the Court of Criminal Appeal in a 1963 case, Ashworth, J., declared that "while it is no doubt right to say in general terms that police constables have a duty to prevent crime and a duty, when crime is committed, to bring the offender to justice, it is also clear from the decided cases that when the execution of these general duties involves interference with the person or property of a private person, the powers of constables are not unlimited." [4]

Under the common law any private person may exercise the power of arrest, without warrant, but this power is limited to cases of treason or felony where the offense was actually committed or attempted in his presence, or where there was immediate danger of the commission of such an offense, or where a breach of the peace has actually been committed or is reasonably apprehended. The arrester may lawfully use whatever force is necessary. The burden of proving the commission of an offense, or reasonable apprehension thereof, is on the person making the arrest. [5] Where there has been a private arrest, it must be established that a felony had actually been committed, or that a reasonable

3. D.P.P. v. Head, [1959] A.C. 83, 106 (H.L.).

4. R. v. Waterfield, [1964] 1 Q.B. 164, [1963] 3 All E.R. 659, 661 (C.C.A.).

5. Walters v. W. H. Smith & Son, Ltd., [1914] 1 K.B. 595.

person would fairly have thought so.[6] After a private arrest has been made, the arrested person must be brought to a magistrate, not "forthwith or immediately," but only "as speedily as is reasonably necessary" in the light of all the circumstances.[7] Furthermore, private arrests are permitted by many modern statutes, such as the Larceny Act, 1916, section 41 (1), the Coinage Offences Act, 1936, section 11, and the Malicious Damage Act, 1861, section 61.[8] In addition, there is a statute that permits the private arrest of anyone who commits an indictable offense at night.[9]

A police officer may, at the common law, arrest without a warrant a person who is reasonably suspected of having committed treason or a felony.[10] The only power of arrest a policeman has, at the common law, that private citizens do not have, is that of lawfully arresting a person on reasonable suspicion even if it turns out that he was mistaken as to both the guilt of the arrested person and the fact that a felony had actually been committed.[11] The constable's common law power of arrest does not extend, however, to non-indictable offenses except for breaches of the peace. "It would be monstrous to say," Lord Campbell, C.J., once wrote, "that, when an assault takes place in the sight of a constable, an officer of the peace, he has not the author-

6. Allen v. Wright (1838) 8 C. & P. 522, 173 E.R. 602 (N.P.) (Tindal, C.J.).

7. John Lewis & Co., Ltd. v. Tims, [1952] A.C. 676, 687 (H.L.).

8. Other statutes authorizing private arrests include the Night Poaching Act, 1828, s. 2; the Vagrancy Act, 1824, s. 6; the Town Police Clauses Act, 1847, s. 15; the Metropolitan Police Act, 1839, s. 66; and the Official Secrets Act, 1911, s. 6.

9. 14 & 15 Vict., c. 19, s. 11 (1851).

10. Hadley v. Perks (1866) L.R. 1 Q.B. 444, 456.

11. Lawrence v. Hedger (1810) 3 Taun. 14, 128 E.R. 6 (C.P.); Beckwith v. Philby (1827) 6 B. & C. 635, 108 E.R. 585 (K.B.).

ity to take the assailant before the magistrate, and cause him to give sureties or be committed." [12] In a recent case [13] the High Court held that a delay of one or two minutes beween the commission of the breach of the peace and the arrest would not warrant the inference that the misdemeanor had not occurred in the presence of the constable. While cycling along the road, the constable saw a man kissing a girl against her will. When the offender walked away, the constable followed him for about ten yards and requested his name and address. When this was refused and the man became offensive, the constable arrested him. The divisional court held that a constable may arrest any person who in his presence commits a misdemeanor or breach of the peace, if the arrest is effected at the time when, or immediately after, the offense is committed, or while there is danger of its renewal.[14] Clearly, "the power to arrest for breach of the peace is limited to an emergency," for when the emergency is over there is nothing to prevent the constable from securing a warrant.[15]

In addition to common law rules on the subject, there are some statutes that confer on the police the power to arrest without a warrant. Usually this power is lim-

12. Derecourt v. Corbishley (1855) 5 E. & B. 188, 193, 119 E.R. 451 (Q.B.).

13. North v. Pullen, *The Times,* Dec. 7, 1961, [1962] Crim. L.R. 97 (Q.B.D.).

14. Timothy v. Simpson (1835) 1 C.M. & R. 757, 149 E.R. 1285 (Ex.), held that a constable who did not witness the breach of the peace may properly arrest the wrongdoer when called on to do so by any person who did see the breach occur.

15. Glanville L. Williams, "Arrest for Breach of the Peace," [1954] Crim. L. Rev. 578, 588. Basically, the American law of arrest follows the English pattern. See Wayne R. LaFave, *Arrest* (Boston: Little, Brown, 1965).

ited to the arrest of persons caught in the act of committing an offense. Otherwise, anyone may be arrested on the charge of having committed any offense on a warrant issued by a judge of the Queen's Bench Division or any justice of the peace.[16] In addition, many statutes authorize the police to make arrests on grounds of reasonable suspicion, e.g., the Offences against the Person Act, 1861, section 66.[17] Pursuant to statute,[18] the Home Secretary issued regulations during World War II [19] authorizing detention of persons he had reasonable grounds to believe had hostile associations, and the House of Lords ruled that a court of law could not inquire whether the Secretary did in fact have reasonable grounds for his belief.[20] Thus in an action for false imprisonment, it was held, the court cannot compel the Secretary to give particulars of the grounds on which he founded his belief. Lord Maugham declared that this was "clearly a matter for executive discretion." [21] He ruled that the Secretary was acting judicially, that he acts on most confidential information, and that he was responsible to Parliament (but not to the courts) for what he does. The House of Lords emphasized the supremacy of Parliament in the English governmental system, which means that Parliament is at liberty, if it

16. Magistrates' Courts Act, 1952, s. 1. Since the adoption of the Criminal Justice Act, 1925, s. 31 (3), a warrant issued by a justice of the peace may be executed anywhere in England or Wales. See D. A. Thomas, "The Execution of Warrants of Arrest," [1962] Crim. L. Rev. 520–31, 597–612.

17. For construction of the Customs Consolidation Act, 1876, s. 186, which authorizes arrest by customs officers, see Barnard v. Gorman, [1941] A.C. 378 (H.L.).

18. Emergency Powers (Defence) Act, 1939.

19. Defence (General) Regulations, 1939, s. 18B.

20. Liversidge v. Anderson, [1942] A.C. 206 (H.L.). To the same effect was a companion case, Greene v. Secretary of State for Home Affairs, [1942] A.C. 284 (H.L.), which came up on habeas corpus.

21. Liversidge v. Anderson, 220.

so desires, to give the Home Secretary an absolute discretion.[22] Even so, Lord Atkin dissented, arguing that it was "one of the pillars of liberty" in English law that "every imprisonment is prima facie unlawful and that it is for a person directing imprisonment to justify his act." [23] He lamented that in a case involving the liberty of the subject the judges had adopted an attitude "more executive minded than the executive." [24]

The House of Lords ruled in 1947 that an arrest without warrant, by police officers, is illegal if the arresting officers give as ground for the arrest a charge of an offense which requires a warrant, even though they thought they had reasonable grounds for believing an offense had been committed that could be the basis of an arrest without warrant.[25] Normally, Viscount Simon said, an arrest without warrant can be justified only if it is on a charge made known to the person arrested. A reason must be given for a warrant, and he could see no reason why this requirement was not equally valid when an arrest is made without a warrant, one practical reason for this being that the person, if informed, may be able to offer an explanation. Lord Simonds,

22. Lord Wright noted that English liberty was "a regulated freedom. It is not an abstract or absolute freedom. Parliament is supreme. . . . In the constitution of this country there are no guaranteed or absolute rights. The safeguard of British liberty is in the good sense of the people and in the system of representative and responsible government which has been evolved. If extraordinary powers are here given, they are given because the emergency is extraordinary and are limited to the period of the emergency." *Id.* at 260–61.

23. *Id.* at 245.

24. *Id.* at 244.

25. Christie v. Leachinsky [1947] A.C. 573 (H.L.). While detention for questioning is illegal under English law, the police continue to engage in this practice. See Glanville L. Williams, "Police Detention and Arrest Privileges: England," 51 J. Crim. L., Crim. and Pol. Sci. 413–18 (1960); Harry Street, *Freedom, the Individual and the Law* (London: Penguin Books, 1963), Chap. 1.

another judge, also added that, since one has a right to resist an unlawful arrest, he cannot know what to do if he is arrested without knowing why.[26] At the same time, it was noted that there are exceptions, as, for example, when the arrested person is caught red-handed, or where other circumstances indicate that he must know the general nature of the alleged offense for which he is detained, or where, by immediate counter-attack or by running away, he makes it practically impossible to be informed.

Finally, it is to be noted that an arrested person is entitled to be charged promptly. Thus the Court of Criminal Appeal recently expressed its strong disapproval of the police holding a man, who had been picked up for drunken driving, for eight hours in jail without charging him.[27] Similarly, a constable who has arrested a man on suspicion of a felony must take him before a justice to be examined as soon as he reasonably can.[28] Furthermore, one who is arrested must be taken to jail by direct road, and if he is sent *extra viam*, a trespass has been committed.[29]

Bail

One of the important privileges of a person accused of a crime in England, though it is a limited one, is that of securing his freedom pending trial, or pending an appeal, by posting bail.[30] Bail may be allowed by a

26. Lord du Parcq pointed out, however, that "the law does not encourage the subject to resist the authority of one whom he knows to be an officer of the law." Christie v. Leachinsky, A.C. 599 (H.L.).

27. R. v. Morgan, *The Times*, June 15, 1961, [1961] Crim. L. Rev. 538 (C.C.A.). The U.S. Supreme Court frowns on long delays between arrest and the bringing of the accused to a magistrate. See McNabb v. United States, 318 U.S. 332 (1943); Mallory v. United States, 354 U.S. 449 (1957).

28. Wright v. Court (1825) 4 B. & C. 596, 107 E.R. 1182 (K.B.).

29. Morris v. Wise (1860) 2 F. & F. 51, 175 E.R. 955 (N.P.).

magistrate, and in cases involving minor offenses, where magistrates are not readily available, bail may be allowed by ranking police officers.[31] The police may also grant bail where a person has been arrested without a warrant and it appears that the investigation will not soon be completed,[32] though this is rarely done. The police may also grant bail where the accused is under the age of seventeen and it is not possible to bring him to a court immediately, whether the arrest was with or without warrant, provided that no serious crime such as homicide is involved and that association with known criminals or prostitutes will not thereby be continued.[33] In all cases except those involving the charge of treason, bail may be granted by examining magistrates.[34] Only a Secretary of State or a judge of the Queen's Bench Division may allow bail in treason cases.[35]

Bail is more available to persons charged with misdemeanors than to persons accused of felonies. Under the common law, the magistrate, in the case of misdemeanors, was obliged to grant bail after the preliminary hearing,[36] but a nineteenth-century statute gave the magistrates discretion where certain misdemeanors, such as obtaining by false pretences, perjury, or riot, were

30. See J. B. Egan, "Bail in Criminal Law," [1959] Crim. L. Rev. 705–14; J. D. Devlin, *Criminal Courts and Procedure* (London: Butterworth, 1960), Chap. 10; Pendleton Howard, *Criminal Justice in England* (New York: Macmillan, 1931), pp. 336–42; T. J. C., "Arresting an Arresting Process," 127 J.P. & L.G. Rev. 3–5 (January 5, 1963); H. A. Palmer and Henry Palmer, *Wilshere's Criminal Procedure* (4th ed.; London: Street & Maxwell, 1961), pp. 40–45.

31. Magistrates' Courts Act, 1952, s. 38 (1).

32. *Ibid.*, s. 38 (2).

33. Children and Young Persons Act, 1933, s. 32 (1).

34. Magistrates' Courts Act, 1952, ss. 7 (2), 8, 95.

35. Magistrates' Courts Act, 1952, s. 8.

36. Marriot's Case (1697) 1 Salk. 104, 91 E.R. 96 (K.B.); R. v. Peatley (1844) 8 J.P. 854 (B.C.); Re Frost (1888) 4 T.L.R. 757 (D.C.).

involved, and where the costs of prosecution could be charged against the administrative county.[37] Since the enactment of the Costs in Criminal Cases Act, 1908, however, all costs in misdemeanor cases may be so charged. If bail is denied in a misdemeanor case, the accused must be informed of his right to apply to a judge of the High Court.[38]

In fact, at the common law the refusal of a justice to grant bail on a charge of misdemeanor is actionable, although it has been held that since the duty to grant bail is judicial, and not ministerial, the court has discretion, and therefore the action is not sustainable without proof of malice or improper motive.[39] As a general rule, one accused of a felony is not entitled to bail as of right.[40] Only under exceptional circumstances is bail granted in treason [41] or murder [42] cases. The High Court has no inherent jurisdiction to grant bail to a convicted person,[43] though it has statutory authority to admit to bail one who has been committed by a magistrates' court to Quarter Sessions for sentence, if the prisoner gives notice of appeal against his conviction.[44] But the Lord Chief Justice, Lord Goddard, said in 1951 that

37. 11 & 12 Vict., c. 42, s. 23.

38. Criminal Justice Administration Act, 1914, s. 23.

39. Linford v. Fitzroy (1849) 13 Q.B.D. 240, 116 E.R. 1255.

40. *Ex parte* Allen (1834) 3 Nev. & Man. 35 (K.B.); R. v. Jones (1843) 2 L.T.O.S. 169, 7 J.P. 741 (Q.B.); R. v. Morris and Mason (1850) 14 J.P. 68 (B.C.); R. v. Stokes (1854) 3 W.R. 10 (Q.B.).

41. Crosby's Case (1695) 12 St. Tr. 1291, 88 E.R. 1167 (K.B.); Witham v. Dutton (1689) Comb. 111, 90 E.R. 374 (K.B.); Kirk's Case (1699) 5 Mod. Rep. 454, 87 E.R. 760 (K.B.).

42. Herbert and Vaughan's Case (1625) Lat. 12, 82 E.R. 249 (K.B.); R. v. Chapman (1838) 8 C. & P. 558, 173 E.R. 617 (Oxford Assizes); *Re* Barthelemy (1852) 1 E. & B. 8, 118 E.R. 340 (Q.B.).

43. *Ex parte* Blyth, [1944] K.B. 532.

44. Magistrates' Courts Act, 1952, ss. 28, 29; Criminal Justice Act, 1948, s. 37 (1) (a).

"such an application is obviously one which ought to be exercised with extreme care," and he added that he hoped "that bail will only be granted in exceptional cases." [45] Generally speaking, bail will not be granted to a prisoner pending his appeal.[46] The Court of Criminal Appeal has discretion to grant bail to an appellant while the appeal is pending,[47] but only in special circumstances,[48] and bail is not granted if there appears to be no prospect of the appellant winning his appeal. For example, bail has been granted to an appellant because of the complexity of the case and the interval of the Long Vacation.[49] On the other hand, bail has been denied pending appeal because it was felt that its purpose was to delay the appeal,[50] or where the term of imprisonment was long.[51] It is in the discretion of the judge to grant or refuse bail when the trial is postponed.[52]

45. *Re* Whitehouse, [1951] 1 K.B. 673, [1951] 1 All E.R. 353.

46. R. v. Gordon (1912) 7 Cr. App. R. 182 (C.C.A.); R. v. Gott (1921) 16 Cr. App. R. 86 (C.C.A.); R. v. Howeson (1936) 25 Cr. App. R. 167 (C.C.A.).

47. Criminal Justice Act, 1948, s. 37; Criminal Appeal Act, 1007, o. 14 (2).

48. R. v. Gregory (1928) 20 Cr. App. R. 185 (C.C.A.); R. v. Greenberg (1923) 17 Cr. App. R. 106 (C.C.A.); R. v. Klein (1932) 23 Cr. App. R. 173 (C.C.A.).

49. R. v. Newbery and Elman (1931) 23 Cr. App. R. 66 (C.C.A.); R. v. Stewart (1931) 23 Cr. App. R. 68 (C.C.A.); R. v. Harding (1931) 23 Cr. App. R. 143 (C.C.A.).

50. R. v. Horner (1910) 4 Cr. App. R. 189 (C.C.A.).

51. R. v. Garnham (1910) 4 Cr. App. R. 150 (C.C.A.). But bail may be granted where the term of imprisonment is short: R. v. Selkirk (1925) 18 Cr. App. R. 172 (C.C.A.).

52. R. v. Osborn (1837) 7 C. & P. 799, 173 E.R. 348 (N.P.); R. v. Owen (1839) 9 C. & P. 83, 173 E.R. 751 (N.P.); R. v. Bridgeman (1830) 4 J.P. 557 (Western Circuit Assizes); R. v. Bourton (1843) 7 J.P. 115 (Wilts Assizes). Basic American rules of law on the subject of bail are very much like those that prevail in Britain. See David Fellman, *The Defendant's Rights* (New York: Rinehart, 1958), pp. 22–29.

English courts will not accept professional bailsmen as sureties, and the bail-bond racket so familiar in the United States is unknown in Britain.[53] Bail must be given by someone who can satisfy the court as to his financial competence; householders are preferred, and persons under twenty-one, bankrupts, and convicted persons are not acceptable. An agreement or contract by the accused to indemnify his bail against the consequences of his own non-appearance is contrary to public policy because in effect it gives the public the security of one person only instead of two people.[54] Under this arrangement, the surety has no interest in seeing to it that the condition of the recognizance is performed.[55] Of course, a magistrate has a right to inquire into the sufficiency and qualifications of a bail, but he is not justified in seeking to persuade or otherwise prevent a person from assisting his neighbor by going bail.[56] Furthermore, where a bail is otherwise sufficient, he ought not to be refused because of his personal character or political opinions.[57] The only test is his sufficiency to answer for the appearance of the party in the amount reasonably required for that purpose. In his discretion, the magistrate may grant bail

53. See Albert Lieck, "Bail Bonds of Surety Companies," 72 Sol. J. 589 (1928).

54. Jones v. Orchard (1855) 16 C.B. 614, 139, E.R. 900 (C.P.); Wilson v. Strugnell (1881) 7 Q.B.D. 548, 14 Cox C.C. 624; Herman v. Jeuchner (1885) 15 Q.B.D. 561, 53 L.T. 94; R. v. Porter, [1910] 1 K.B. 369.

55. Consolidated Exploration and Finance Co. v. Musgrave, [1900] 1 Ch. 37, 81 L.T. 747, 16 T.L.R. 13.

56. R. v. Saunders (1847) 2 Cox. C.C. 249 (Q.B.D.).

57. R. v. Badger (1843) 4 Q.B. 468, 114 E.R. 975. Two persons proposed as bail had been turned down because they had attended Chartist meetings.

without any sureties if he believes that justice will not thereby be defeated.[58]

The Bill of Rights, 1688, specifically forbids excessive bail. A judge of the High Court has no inherent jurisdiction to reduce the amount of bail as fixed by justices in the exercise of their statutory powers,[59] but where justices have demanded excessive bail, a petition to the divisional court for a writ of habeas corpus is a proper, though a very unusual, procedure.[60] There have also been cases where the divisional court has remitted a case with an instruction to admit to bail.[61]

Generally speaking, the controlling principle in granting bail is not the supposed guilt or innocence of the accused, but rather the probability of his appearing for trial.[62] In making this decision, however, the justices exercise a discretionary authority, and they may take into account various considerations, including the nature of the offense, the strength of the evidence, the gravity of the punishment on conviction, the character and behavior of the accused, his previous criminal record, his economic circumstances, the reliability of the sureties, and the danger of the defendant's tampering with the witnesses if freed.[63] In addition, magistrates take into account the attitude of the police and whether the accused is employed and has dependents.

---

58. Bail Act, 1898, s. 1.

59. *Ex parte* Speculand, [1946] K.B. 48.

60. *Ex parte* Thomas, [1956] Crim. L. Rev. 119 (Q.B.).

61. R. v. Manning (1888) 5 T.L.R. 139 (Q.B.).

62. R. v. Scaife (1841) 9 Dowl. 553, 5 J.P. 406 (B.C.).

63. R. v. Rudd (1775) 1 Cowp. 331, 98 E.R. 1114 (K.B.); R. v. Barront and Allain (1852) 1 E. & B. 1, 118 E.R. 337 (Q.B.); *Re* Robinson (1854) 23 L.J.Q.B. 286, 2 W.R. 424; R. v. Rose (1898) 67 L.J.Q.B. 289, 292 (C.C.R.); H. M. Advocate v. Saunders, [1913] S.C. (J.) 44; R. v Fletcher (1949) 113 J.P. 365 (C.C.A.).

The Court of Criminal Appeal has recently stressed that it is inadvisable to grant bail to a person who has a long criminal record unless there is very real doubt as to his guilt.[64] Not long ago this court called attention to the fact that, while on bail, a young housebreaker with a long criminal record committed nine additional offenses.[65] Atkinson, J., declared: "In cases of felony, bail is discretionary, and the matters which ought to be taken into consideration include the nature of the accusation, the nature of the evidence in support of the accusation, and the severity of the punishment which conviction will entail. Some crimes are not at all likely to be repeated pending trial and in those cases there may be no objection to bail; but some are, and housebreaking particularly is a crime which will very probably be repeated if a prisoner is released on bail, especially in the case of a man who has a record for housebreaking such as the applicant had."

In deciding whether or not to grant bail, magistrates are heavily influenced by the attitude of the police. A Home Office study of the conduct of magistrates' courts during 1957 indicated that the police opposed bail for 38 per cent of the persons committed for trial, for 21 per cent of the persons finally dealt with by the magistrates, and for 48 per cent of the persons committed for sentence.[66] The weight of the police's recommendations is reflected in the fact that only two per cent of those remanded or committed were granted bail after police opposition was expressed. But the position of the

64. R. v. Pegg, [1955] Crim. L. Rev. 308 (C.C.A.); R. v. Wharton, [1955] Crim. L. Rev. 565 (C.C.A.); R. v. Gentry, [1956] Crim. L. Rev. 120 (C.C.A.).

65. R. v. Phillips (1947) 32 Cr. App. R. 47 (C.C.A.).

66. Evelyn Gibson, *Time Spent Awaiting Trial*, Home Office Research Unit Report (London: H.M.S.O., 1960), p. 32.

police has not always been so decisive, as is reflected in the fact that three per cent were remanded or committed in custody although the police had stated that they had no objection to bail, and 13 per cent were not granted bail although the police had given no views on the subject. The study also indicated that persons on bail were more likely to have dependents than those in custody, apparently because men with dependents are more likely to obtain or keep employment.[67] But it was suggested that possibly such people are likely to be of a different type.

An eminent authority on English criminal law, a former chief inspector of the City of London Police, has recently recommended several changes in the law and practice relating to bail.[68] He thinks that the method of getting bail should be simplified and speeded up, that undefended persons should have the aid of counsel on the question of bail, that police should be ready to give full reasons, supported by affidavit, for opposing the grant of bail, that the court should always give its reasons for refusing bail, and that more judges should be available to handle requests for bail. He also writes that "the powers possessed by the police are so great that they are able to use the threat of opposing bail as a weapon for procuring information from a prisoner. Some

67. Gibson, *Time Spent Awaiting Trial*, p. 33.

68. C. H. Rolph, "Criminal Law," in *Law Reform Now*, Gerald Gardiner and Andrew Martin, eds. (London: Victor Gollancz, 1963), pp. 252–56. There is a great deal of interest in the United States in bail reform, as indicated by the report of the Attorney General's Committee on Poverty and the Administration of Criminal Justice, *Poverty and the Administration of Criminal Justice* (Washington: Government Printing Office, 1963), Chap. 3, and the National Conference on Bail and Criminal Justice, held in May, 1964. See "A Study of the Administration of Bail in New York City," 106 U. Pa. L. Rev. 693–730 (March, 1958).

police officers can be vindictive if defendants refuse to co-operate with them. Although the police do not as a body abuse their powers, there are too many individual instances of abuse." [69]

Prosecution

From the point of view of American practice, the absence of grand juries [70] and of the Tom Dewey type of full-time professional prosecuting attorneys, as well as the initiation of criminal prosecutions by private parties, are the chief items of interest in the English concept of criminal prosecution. In the absence of a statutory provision to the contrary, any private citizen may on his own initiative start criminal proceedings by instructing counsel. But the Director of Public Prosecutions, if he chooses to do so, may at any stage take over any private prosecution,[71] and the Attorney-General can stop a prosecution at any stage of the proceedings, in his absolute discretion, by entering a nolle prosequi.[72] There are not many private prosecutions these days, and they are chiefly in the commercial field. Most criminal cases are

69. Rolph, "Criminal Law." p. 255.

70. The grand jury was abolished by the Administration of Justice Act, 1933, s. 1 (1). The High Court ruled in R. v. Rhodes, [1899] 1 Q.B. 77 (C.C.R.), that section 1 of the Criminal Evidence Act, 1898, did not confer upon the accused the right to give evidence before the grand jury. The statute provided: "Every person charged with an offence . . . shall be a competent witness for the defence at every stage of the proceedings." The court held that a grand jury had nothing to do with the defense; it sat in private and heard only the prosecution's evidence.

71. See Prosecution of Offences Act, 1908, s. 2. (3), and Duchesne v. Finch (1912) 28 T.L.R. 440 (K.B.). Corporations may prosecute. In the eighteenth and nineteenth centuries there were private prosecution societies, but they have disappeared.

72. Glanville L. Williams, "The Power to Prosecute," [1955] Crim. L. Rev. 596–604, 668–97.

prosecuted by the police,[73] except that the Director of Public Prosecutions must take over every murder case and may take over other cases, such as cases involving sedition, conspiracy to defeat justice, coinage offenses, etc., if the general public interest is served thereby. In addition, many prosecutions are initiated by government departments pursuant to statutory authority. For example, the Post Office Department brings prosecutions for offenses under the Post Office Act, the Ministry of Labour is involved in prosecutions relating to factory legislation, and the Board of Trade is concerned with cases involving such matters as weights and measures, bankruptcies, and companies. Some departments have their own prosecuting staffs, and the Director of Public Prosecutions looks after the needs of those that do not. As in the United States, malicious prosecution without reasonable and proper cause is an actionable wrong.[74]

Statutes set forth various rules regarding the prosecution of criminal cases. According to Parliamentary decree, many crimes can be prosecuted only at the direction of or with the consent of some public official, such as the Home Secretary, a law officer of the Crown, the Director of Public Prosecutions, a policeman, or a local official. Thus, the consent of the Attorney-General is needed for prosecuting offenses under the Coinage Offences Act, 1936, section 4 (3), and the Public Order Act, 1936, sections 1 (2) and 2 (2). Prosecutions under the Dangerous Drugs Act, 1951, section 18 (1) (a) re-

---

73. During 1960, counsel in the Solicitor's Department of the Metropolitan Police handled 9,015 cases at courts of trial and at courts of summary jurisdiction; members of the staff handled 4,170. Report of the Commissioner of Police of the Metropolis for the Year 1960, 1961, Cmd. 1440, p. 38.

74. Glinski v. McIver, [1962] A.C. 726 (H.L.). See Joseph Yahuda, "Malicious Prosecution," 107 Sol. J. 6–9 (1963).

quire the leave of the Director of Public Prosecutions. Prosecutions for violating the Customs and Excise Act, 1952, section 281 (1) (3), require the consent of the customs commissioners or other law officers of the Crown. The Postmaster-General must give his consent in regard to certain offenses under the Post Office Act, 1953, sections 56 (3) and 63 (3). One statute, the Law of Libel Amendment Act, 1888, section 8, provides that a criminal libel action against a newspaper can be started only by order of a judge.[75]

The office of the Director of Public Prosecutions was created by act of Parliament in 1879,[76] and after it was abolished in 1884 [77] it was recreated as a separate department in 1908.[78] While the Director is appointed by the Home Secretary, with the concurrence of the Prime Minister and after consultation with the Attorney-General, he is actually under the supervision of the Attorney-General. There is close liaison between the Home Office and the Director of Public Prosecutions in criminal matters, but the Home Secretary is not responsible for and does not give instructions to the Director. As a matter of fact, the Home Secretary no longer has any significant concern with prosecutions, as he once did. The Home Office has a great deal to do, of course, with

75. The Vexatious Actions Act, 1896, s. 1, provides that the Attorney-General may, in the case of one who has "habitually and persistently instituted legal proceedings without any reasonable ground," apply to the High Court for an order that will require the person to get leave to sue from a judge of the High Court, who must be shown that there is a prima-facie ground for the proceeding. The High Court has ruled, however, that the term "legal proceedings" does not include criminal proceedings. *In re* Vexatious Actions Act, 1896, [1914] 1 K.B. 122.

76. Prosecution of Offences Act, 1879.

77. Prosecution of Offences Act, 1884.

78. Prosecution of Offences Act, 1908. The statute separated the department from the office of the Treasury Solicitor.

the criminal law and the functioning of the courts, but it is not a prosecuting authority or a Ministry of Justice.[79] The Attorney-General, however, in his judicial capacity is independent of the government, and he has the authority, by entering a nolle prosequi, to dismiss any case except summary cases, which require leave of the court.[80]

The Director of Public Prosecutions has a variety of functions. It is his duty to institute and carry on criminal proceedings in any case where the offense is punishable with death, in cases involving offenses against the coinage, in any case referred to him by a government department in which he thinks criminal proceedings should be instituted, or in any case he thinks is important or difficult or which, for any other reason, requires his intervention.[81] He is obliged to prosecute on the order of the Attorney-General or a secretary of state. He has discretion to take over any private prosecution, though he will not usually do so where the prosecution is instituted by a bank or wealthy commercial house.[82] There are certain types of cases which must be reported to the Director for possible action on his part, such as those involving offenses that affect the whole community (e.g., sedition, conspiracy to defeat

79. See Sir Frank Newsam, *The Home Office* (London: Allen & Unwin, 1954), pp. 134–36.

80. See Lord MacDermott, *Protection from Power under English Law* (London: Stevens, 1957), pp. 35–36.

81. The basic statute, Prosecution of Offences Act, 1879, s. 2, provides that he may direct prosecutions "in cases which appear to be of importance or difficulty, or in which special circumstances, or the refusal or failure of a person to proceed with a prosecution, appear to render the action of such Director necessary to secure the due prosecution of an offender. . . ."

82. Sir Maurice Amos, *British Criminal Justice* (rev. ed.; London: Longmans, Green, 1957). p. 29.

justice, corruption of or by a public official) or other serious offenses (e.g., manslaughter, rape, obscene libels), cases where prosecution has been abandoned or withdrawn, extradition cases, and cases involving corrupt or illegal election practices. In addition, he has the duty of managing the Crown's defense in most appeals taken to the Court of Criminal Appeal.

The Director has other duties besides those relating to prosecutions. He gives advice, on his own initiative or on application, to government departments, to clerks to the justices, coroners, chief police officers, and to others, either orally or in writing. A former Director has written that "this is in many respects the most important part of the work of the Director. . . ." [83] An American observer has pointed out that the office of the Director "has, in fact, of late years become very much like a central bureau of legal information for the police." [84]

The Director of Public Prosecutions is by no means the only public prosecutor of England, and his department does not investigate crime.[85] His power to prosecute is largely discretionary, and in fact his department conducts a relatively small percentage of all prosecutions. For example, in 1948 he prosecuted only 487 out of 671,000 persons dealt with summarily, and only 900 out of 22,750 persons dealt with at Quarter Sessions and Assizes.[86] In 1955 the Director undertook only 989 prosecutions for indictable offenses out of a total of

83. Sir Theobald Mathew, *The Office and Duties of the Director of Public Prosecutions* (London: University of London Press, 1950), p. 13. See also Prosecution of Offences Regulations, 1946 (S.R. & O. 1946, No. 1467/L17).

84. Howard, *Criminal Justice in England,* p. 110.

85. Sir Edward Tindal Atkinson, "The Department of the Director of Public Prosecutions," 22 Can. B. Rev. 413–21 (1944).

86. Mathew, *The Office and Duties,* p. 4.

114,811, and only 115 prosecutions for non-indictable offenses.[87]

It remains to be noted that, as Lord Devlin has observed, "the last half-century has seen a welcome transition in the role of prosecuting counsel from a persecuting advocate into a 'minister of justice,'"[88] for English judges insist that the prosecutor be fair to the point of assisting the defense.[89] "In England today," Lord Denning has written, "every counsel who is instructed for the prosecution knows how essential it is to be fair. The country expects it. The judges require it. He must not press for a conviction. If he knows of a point in favour of the prisoner, he must bring it out. He must state the facts quite dispassionately, whether they tell in favour of a severe sentence or otherwise. No counsel would dream of doing otherwise. Likewise with the right of cross-examinination, counsel for the prosecution must exercise it in a moderate and restrained manner, not in any way browbeating the man who is on trial."[90]

87. Amos, *British Criminal Justice*, p. 29.

88. Sir Patrick Devlin, *Trial by Jury* (London: Stevens, 1956), p. 122. The phrase is that of Avory, J., in R. v. Banks (1916) 12 Cr. App. R. 74, 76 (C.C.A.).

89. Christmas Humphreys, "The Duties and Responsibilities of Prosecuting Counsel," [1955] Crim. L. Rev. 739–48. Cf. Brady v. Maryland, 373 U.S. 83 (1963).

90. Sir Alfred Denning, *The Road to Justice* (London: Stevens, 1955), pp. 36–37. The U.S. Supreme Court takes the same position. See Berger v. United States, 295 U.S. 78, 88 (1935); and Viereck v. United States, 318 U.S. 236, 247 (1943).

III

The Police and the Accused

Police Interrogation

IN AN opinion published in 1961, Justice Frankfurter called attention to the fastidious standards observed by English courts in dealing with the important question of police interrogation.[1] He noted the fact that "the English courts have long tended severely to discourage law enforcement officers from asking questions of persons under arrest or who are so far suspected that their arrest is imminent."[2] The position of English judges on this subject was formulated many years ago. In October, 1906, the chief constable of Birmingham, through the

1. Culombe v. Connecticut, 367 U.S. 568, 593–98 (1961).

2. *Id.* at 593. While police interrogation is routine in the United States, in recent years the U.S. Supreme Court has recognized some limitations on the police in this respect. Thus, in a recent case, Escobedo v. Illinois, 378 U.S. 478 (1964), the court ruled that where a general investigation is no longer going on, and the police have focused on the accused as a suspect, denial of his request to consult with his attorney before submitting to any further questioning is a violation of due process of law. Cf. Massiah v. United States, 377 U.S. 201 (1964); Crooker v. California, 357 U.S. 433 (1958). There is great uncertainty in state law as to whether the police must first warn a suspect of his rights before questioning him. See Wayne R. LaFave, *Arrest* (Boston: Little, Brown, 1965), pp. 388–98.

Home Office, sought the advice of the judges of the High Court regarding the duty of constables to caution prisoners in their custody before asking questions. Lord Alverstone, the Lord Chief Justice, wrote a reply on behalf of the judges, and out of further consultations among them there emerged in 1912 the first formulation of the so-called Judges' Rules, then four in number.[3] In 1918 the number of Judges' Rules was increased to nine,[4] and, following criticism by a Royal Commission,[5] the Home Office in 1930 issued a clarifying circular with the approval of the judges.[6] The Lord Chief Justice approved additional Home Office circulars in 1947 and 1948.[7] On March 16, 1961, in response to a question raised in the House of Commons, Mr. R. A. Butler, the Home Secretary, announced that the Lord Chief Justice agreed with him that it was then appropriate for the judges to review the scope and operation of the rules.[8] After extensive study by a committee of judges, and approval by a meeting of the judges of Queen's Bench, a set of revised rules was adopted and announced by the Home Office in January, 1964.[9]

3. For the text see R. v. Voisin, [1918] 1 K.B. 531, 539 n. (3); R. v. Cook (1918) 34 T.L.R. 515 (C.C.A.).

4. See "Statements by Suspects and Prisoners" (1918) 145 L.T. 389.

5. Report of the Royal Commission on Police Powers and Procedure, 1929, Cmd. 3297, pp. 69–74.

6. See Barrister, "Prisoners' Statements," 6 Pol. J. 342, 352–56 (1933); 1 *Taylor on Evidence* (12th ed. 1931), 557 59.

7. For the full text of the rules at this date, see Stone's *Justices' Manual* (92nd ed. 1960), pp. 353–56; Sir Patrick Devlin, *The Criminal Prosecution in England* (New Haven: Yale University Press, 1958), pp. 137–41.

8. 636 H.C. Deb., Hansard, No. 75, 1961 (written answers) col. 145.

9. Home Office Circular No. 31/1964. For the text of the new rules, see "The Judges' Rules and Administrative Directions to the Police,"

As Justice Frankfurter noted, "the Judges' Rules are not 'law' in the sense that any violation of them by a questioning officer eo ipso renders inadmissible in evidence whatever incriminatory responses he may obtain."[10] This point is well established in English decisional law. Thus the Court of Criminal Appeal, through A. T. Lawrence, J., ruled in a leading case on the subject that a statement made voluntarily by a prisoner was, in the discretion of the judge, admissible even though the caution prescribed by the Judges' Rules had not been given.[11] For, said the Court, "these rules have not the force of law; they are administrative directions the observance of which the police authorities should enforce upon their subordinates as tending to the fair administration of justice. It is important that they should do so, for statements obtained from prisoners, contrary to the spirit of these rules, may be rejected as evidence by the judge presiding at the trial."[12] Though it has often been pointed out by courts that the Judges' Rules do not have the force of law,[13] it is equally true that trial judges have a wide discretion and may exclude admissions secured in violation of the Judges' Rules.[14] On the other hand, if circumstances warrant,

[1964] Crim. L. Rev. 165–73; Gerald Abrahams, *Police Questioning and the Judges' Rules* (London: Oyez Publications, 1964), pp. 52–60.

10. Culombe v. Connecticut, 367 U.S. at 596–97.

11. R. v. Voisin [1918] 1 K.B. 531, 13 Cr. App. R. 89, 26 Cox C.C. 224 (C.C.A.).

12. [1918] 1 K.B. at 539–40.

13. R. v. Wattam (1952) 36 Cr. App. R. 72, 77 (C.C.A.); R. v. Straffen, [1952] 2 Q.B. 911, 914 (C.C.A.); R. v. Sargeant, [1963] Crim. L. Rev. 848 (C.C.A.); R. v. Powell-Mantle, [1959] Crim. L. Rev. 445 (Bedford. Q. Sess.); R. v. Williamson, [1964] Crim. L. Rev. 126 (C.C.A.).

14. R. v. Dwyer (1932) 23 Cr. App. R. 156 (C.C.A.); R. v. Bass (1953) 37 Cr. App. R. 51, [1953] 1 Q.B. 680 (C.C.A.). See Ian Brownlie, "Police Questioning, Custody and Caution," [1960] Crim. L. Rev. 298–324.

evidence secured without observance of the Judges' Rules may, in the court's discretion, be admitted.[15] For example, the Court of Criminal Appeal recently upheld a conviction even though a statement had been secured by the police in "flagrant" violation of one of the Judges' Rules because it was felt that the jury would have come to the same conclusion without the statement.[16]

The Judges' Rules are based on the assumption that since an arrested person is under the pressure of a situation that is essentially coercive, the police must not urge him to prove his own guilt. "The courts," it has been observed, "acting on long experience, make the assumption that a majority of persons, especially ignorant persons, and especially persons under anxiety, find it difficult not to talk to a questioner whose personality and function are psychologically impressive." [17] Long before the first Judges' Rules were formulated, English courts took the position that after a person has been arrested, or after the constable has made up his mind to charge a person with the commission of a crime, no further questions of any sort can be put without first cautioning him that he is not obliged to answer and that anything he says may be used in evidence.[18] Repeatedly and emphatically, English judges ruled that the police do not have the authority, even after a caution, to question or cross-examine an accused person who has been taken into custody, for since a magistrate

15. R. v. Voisin, [1918] 1 K.B. 531 (C.C.A.); R. v. Smith (1961) 46 Cr. App. R. 51, [1962] Crim. L. Rev. 38, [1961] 3 All E.R. 972 (C.C.A.); R. v. Massey (1963) 107 S.J. 984, [1964] Crim. L. Rev. 43 (C.C.A.).

16. R. v. Kennedy, Steele and Meakin, [1963] Crim. L. Rev. 108 (C.C.A.).

17. Abrahams, *Police Questioning*, pp. 8–9.

18. R. v. Histed (1898) 19 Cox C.C. 16 (Lewes Assizes); R. v. Kerr (1837) 8 C. & P. 176, 173 E.R. 449 (N.P.); R. v. Regan (1867) 17 L.T.R.N.S. 325 (N.P.).

or judge cannot question the prisoner,[19] "a police officer
certainly has no more right to do so." [20] A constable was
permitted to ask questions of a person not yet charged [21]
or taken into custody,[22] but once the suspect was in
custody the police officer had no authority to cross-
examine him,[23] though he could ask him to explain,
after a caution, such matters as possession on his person
of certain property.[24]

In a well-known dissenting opinion published in 1864,
a judge, in objecting to police interrogation, called attention to the relative positions of the accused and the
police, and to "the ordinary infirmities of mankind." [25]
He wrote: "The danger to be guarded against is not, in
the far greatest number of cases, that an innocent man
will fabricate a statement of his own guilt, although
instances of this have occurred, too well attested to be

19. See R. v. Pettit (1850) 4 Cox C.C. 164, 165 (Essex Assizes).
Said Wilde, C.J. "The law is so extremely cautious in guarding against
anything like torture, that it extends a similar principle to every case
where a man is not a free agent in meeting an inquiry. If this sort of
examination be admitted in evidence, it is hard to say where it might
stop."

20. R. v. Knight and Thayre (1905) 20 Cox C.C. 711, 21 T.L.R.
310 (Lewes Assizes). See also R. v. Gavin (1885) 15 Cox C.C. 656
(Liverpool Assizes); R. v. Male and Cooper (1893) 17 Cox C.C. 689
(Stafford Assizes); R. v. Mick (1863) 3 F. & F. 822, 176 E.R. 376
(York Assizes); R. v. Day (1847) 11 J.P. 245, 2 Cox C.C. 209 (Win-
chester Assizes); R. v. Morgan (1895) 59 J.P. 827 (Birmingham Assizes).

21. R. v. Miller (1895) 18 Cox C.C. 54 (Liverpool Assizes); R. v.
Liebling (1909) 2 Cr. App. R. 314 (C.C.A.); R. v. Berriman (1854)
6 Cox C.C. 388 (Surrey Assizes).

22. R. v. Brackenbury (1893) 17 Cox C.C. 628 (Lincoln Assizes);
R. v. Booth and Jones (1910) 5 Cr. App. R. 177 (C.C.A.).

23. R. v. Winkel (1912) 76 J.P. 191 (C.C.A.); R. v. Gardner and
Hancox (1915) 11 Cr. App. R. 267 (C.C.A.).

24. R. v. Best, [1909] 1 K.B. 692 (C.C.A.).

25. R. v. Johnston (1864) 15 Ir.C.L.R. 60, 121–22 (Cr. App.)
(Pigot, J.).

doubted: the danger is, that an innocent person suddenly arrested, and questioned by one having the power to detain or set free, will—when subjected to interrogatories which *may* be administered in the mildest, or *may* be administered in the harshest way, and to persons of the strongest and boldest, or of the most feeble and nervous natures—make statements not consistent with truth, in order to escape from the pressure of the moment. A prisoner so circumstanced may not hear, in terms, one word of hope held out or of mischief threatened; and yet he may, and in many cases must, be actuated by hope that his answers will lead to his liberation, or fear that his answers may cause his detention in custody. He is placed in immediate contact with one who for the time is his gaoler, for the most part with no third person present to witness what passes, and almost always without the presence of any person to whom he can appeal for protection, or who may control the examination within fair or reasonable bounds. Manner may menace and cause fear as much as words. Manner may insinuate hope as well as verbal assurances. The very act of questioning is in itself an indication that the questioner will or may liberate the answerer if the answers are satisfactory, and detain him if they are not." The judge noted that if, after giving the caution, the constable then goes on to put searching interrogatories, he thereby virtually and in effect abandons the caution, for the process of questioning "impresses, on the greater part of mankind, the belief that silence will be taken as an assent to what the questions imply." Thus the prisoner is deprived of his free agency, and he feels impelled to answer "from the fear of the consequences of declining to do so."

The 1964 edition of the Judges' Rules begins by restating some general principles: "that citizens have a duty to help a police officer to discover and apprehend offenders"; [26] that a police officer cannot compel any person against his will to come to or remain in a police station otherwise than by arrest; [27] that at "any stage of the investigation" a person has a right to communicate and consult privately with a solicitor; that a police officer should charge an offense without delay; and that it is a fundamental condition of admissibility in evidence that statements shall have been voluntary, and not obtained "by fear of prejudice or hope of advantage" on the part of any person in authority, or by "oppression."

Rule 1 states, "When a police officer is trying to discover whether,[28] or by whom, an offence [29] has been committed he is entitled to question any person, whether suspected or not, from whom he thinks that useful information may be obtained. This is so whether or not the person in question has been taken into custody [30] so long as he has not been charged with the offence or informed that he may be prosecuted for it." Thus, while the police may ask questions, there is no necessity for them to caution a person before they have charged him or made up their minds to charge him so long as his

26. See Sykes v. D.P.P., [1962] A.C. 528 (H.L.).

27. Under English law, the police have no right to detain for questioning. Tims v. John Lewis & Co., [1951] 2 K.B. 459. The constable has the choice of either arresting on a charge or accepting the refusal to answer.

28. The phrase relating to the determination of whether an offense has been committed is new; the old rules referred only to discovering "the author of a crime."

29. The old rules used the words "crime;" "offence" is a broader term.

30 It has been held that "custody" means custody of the police, and does not apply to Broadmoor patients. R. v. Straffen, [1952] 2 Q.B. 911 (C.C.A.).

responses are voluntary. For, as was said in a leading decision, "it is desirable in the interests of the community that investigations into crime should not be cramped." [31] Both the old and the new rules permit the questioning of a man in custody about offenses other than that for which he is in custody.[32]

Rule 2 provides, however, that "As soon as a police officer has evidence which would afford reasonable grounds for suspecting that a person has committed an offence, he shall caution that person or cause him to be cautioned before putting to him any questions, or further questions, relating to that offence." [33] The old rule spoke of the officer making up his mind; the new rule has the more objective test of the existence of enough evidence to constitute reasonable grounds for a belief. New Rule 2 also provides the language of the caution: "You are not obliged to say anything unless you wish to do so but what you say may be put into writing and given in evidence." If, after a caution, a person is questioned, or elects to make a statement, then Rule 2 provides that a record shall be kept of the time and place and of the persons present. In connection with this early stage in the investigation, it is worth noting that there is nothing in the Judges' Rules which would prevent the police from taking a person's fingerprints,

31. R. v. Voisin, [1918] 1 K.B. 531, 538, 13 Cr. App. R. 89, 26 Cox C.C. 224 (C.C.A.). See also R. v. Cook (1918) 34 T.L.R. 515 (C.C.A.); Lewis v. Harris (1913) 78 J.P. 68 (K.B.D.); Hennell v. Cuthbert, [1962] Crim. L. Rev. 104 (Q.B.D.); Berry v. Robson, [1964] Crim. L. Rev. 401 (Q.B.D.); R. v. Wattam (1952) 36 Cr. App. R. 72 (C.C.A.).

32. R. v. Buchan, [1964] 1 W.L.R. 365, [1964] 1 All E.R. 502 (C.C.A.).

33. If a person in custody blurts out his confession, the police cannot be expected to caution him. R. v. Sargeant, [1963] Crim. L. Rev. 848 (C.C.A.).

without a caution, since this involves neither answers to questions by the police nor statements.[34]

While the police, though only after a caution, may continue to question a person concerning whom they have evidence in an amount sufficient to justify suspecting that he committed an offense, a different situation exists when a person has been charged or told he may be prosecuted for an offense. Then, says Rule 3, "it is only in exceptional cases that questions relating to the offence should be put to the accused person," and only after a caution.[35] "Such questions may be put where they are necessary for the purpose of preventing or minimising harm or loss to some other person or to the public or for clearing up an ambiguity in a previous answer or statement." At this point the answers "must be contemporaneously recorded in full and the record signed" by the accused, or if he refuses, by the interrogating officer. In addition, a record must be kept of the time and place at which the questioning or statement began and ended, and of the persons present.

This formulation of Rule 3 clarifies the previous Rule 3, which read, "Persons in custody should not be questioned without the usual caution being first administered." Rule 3 "had long been felt to be a trap because there was contemplated that, once cautioned, a person could then be asked questions about his complicity in

34. Callis v. Gunn, [1963] 3 All E.R. 677, [1964] 1 Q.B. 495 (Q.B.D.). Similarly, the Judges' Rules do not forbid eavesdropping by the police; they may report on what they hear. R. v. Mills, [1962] 3 All E.R. 298 (C.C.A.).

35. It is interesting to note, by way of contrast, that under Scottish law the police are not permitted, after arrest, to conduct any interrogation whatsoever. See Chalmers v. H.M. Advocate, [1954] Sess. Cas. 66 (J.C.); T. B. Smith, "Public Interest and the Interests of the Accused in the Criminal Process—Reflections of a Scottish Lawyer," 33 Tul. L. Rev. 349, 360 (1958).

a crime." [36] Thus the Home Office issued a circular in 1930, with the approval of the judges,[37] stating that Rule 3 was not intended to authorize the questioning of people in custody, even if they had been cautioned. Lord Chief Justice Parker observed in 1963 that it was only "in exceptional circumstances" that questions might be put to prisoners in custody after a caution has been given.[38] The 1930 circular of the Home Office pointed out, for example, that before a person had been formally charged with burglary, he may have said that he had hidden or thrown the property away. In this case, after caution, the police may ask him where he had hidden or thrown the property.

Rule 4 relates to the manner of taking written statements after caution. Rule 5 provides that after a person has been charged, and the police wish to show him a statement by another person who has been charged with the same offense, this must be done without saying or doing anything to invite any comment or reply. If the individual then wishes to make a statement in reply, he must at once be cautioned.[39] Rule 6 makes it clear that the rules apply, "so far as may be practicable," to persons other than police officers who are con-

36. R. v. Massey (1963) 107 S.J. 984, 985, (1964) 28 J. Crim. L. 23 (C.C.A.).

37. Home Office Circular, June 24, 1930, No. 536053/23; Stone's *Justices' Manual* (92nd. ed. 1960), p. 365.

38. R. v. Massey, *supra*, note 36. See also R. v. Williamson, *The Times,* Nov. 27, 1963, (1964) 28 J. Crim. L. 24 (C.C.A.); R. v. Parman (1963) 107 Sol. J. 557, 28 J. Crim. L. 32 (C.C.A.); R. v. Thomas and Cullen, [1961] Crim. L. Rev. 401 (Swansea Bor. Q. Sess.); R. v. Powell-Mantle, [1959] Crim. L. Rev. 445 (Bedford. Q. Sess.).

39. In R. v. Gardner and Hancox (1915) 11 Cr. App. R. 265 (C.C.A.), the court condemned the police practice of playing a statement by one prisoner against that of another. See also R. v. Williamson, [1964] Crim. L. Rev. 126 (C.C.A.).

cerned with investigating offenses or charging offenders.

A competent student of the subject has observed that for the most part the new rules amount to an acceptance of current police practices, and that they do not impose much in the way of new restrictions or controls upon the freedom of police questioners.[40] On the other hand, an unidentified police officer writing in the March 1964 issue of the *Criminal Law Review* has argued that the new rules are very vague, that they have been received "with a singular lack of enthusiasm," and that lawyers will no doubt have "plenty of honest fun" in the courts for many years to come trying to give them the meaning they wish.[41] J. C. Smith, Professor of Law at Nottingham, believes that "though the new Rules clear up some points they leave others unresolved, and they clearly raise new problems of their own." [42] But he also believes that they reflect a tendency of the judges to tighten up on the enforcement of the rules. It is an old complaint that the courts are inconsistent in requiring police adherence to the rules, and that the rules are inadequate because they relate solely to the taking of statements that are to be tendered as evidence in court.[43] Furthermore, a committee of *Justice,* the British section of the International Commission of Jurists, pointed out in a 1960 report that the safeguards of the Judges' Rules enter into the procedure at too late a time.[44] The

40. Abrahams, *Police Questioning*, p. 52.

41. Police Officer, "The Judges' Rules and the Police," [1964] Crim. L. Rev. 173, 174.

42. J. C. Smith, "The New Judges' Rules—a Lawyer's View," [1964] Crim. L. Rev. 176, 181.

43. C. H. Rolph, *Common Sense about Crime and Punishment* (London: Victor Gollancz, 1961), pp. 84–91.

44. Justice, *Report on Preliminary Investigations of Criminal Offences* (London: Stevens, 1960), pp. 3–9.

new rules tend to enlarge upon this tendency. One may well agree with the observation of an English legal scholar that it is difficult to find a correct balance between the needs of the police and the requirements of a fair trial.[45]

Confessions

It is an ancient and fundamental principle of English law, and equally basic in American law, that a confession is admissible in evidence only if it is voluntary.[46] As early as 1783 an English court declared: "A confession forced from the mind by the flattery of hope or the torture of fear comes in so questionable a shape when it is to be considered as evidence of guilt that no credit ought to be given to it." [47] Thus it is well established that a confession is admissible in evidence only if the prosecution proves beyond reasonable doubt that it was voluntary.[48] That is to say, the burden of proof is on the prosecution to satisfy the jury that the statement was voluntary.[49] This is an exception to the general rule

45. Ian Brownlie, "Police Questioning, Custody and Caution," [1960] Crim. L. Rev. 298. See also Glanville Williams, "Questioning by the Police—Some Practical Considerations," [1960] Crim. L. Rev. 325. For a brief summary of complaints about police violation of the Judges' Rules see Final Report, Royal Commission on the Police, 1962, Cmd. 1728, paras. 368–70. See also *Inquiry in Regard to the Interrogation by the Police of Miss Savidge*, Report of the Tribunal Appointed under the Tribunals of Inquiry (Evidence) Act, 1921, Cmd. 3147, and 217 H.C. Deb. 1216–20, 1303 39, 1921–31 (Hansard's 5th Ser. 1928).

46. 4 Bl. Com. 296. See Townsend v. Sain, 372 U.S. 293 (1963).

47. R. v. Warickshall (1783) 1 Leach 263, 168 E.R. 234 (C.C.).

48. R. v. Cave, [1963] Crim. L. Rev. 371 (C.C.A.); R. v. Warringham (1851) 2 Den. 447, n., 169 E.R. 575 (C.C.).

49. R. v. Francis and Murphy (1959) 43 Cr. App. R. 174 (C.C.A.); J. A. Andrews, "Involuntary Confessions and Illegally Obtained Evidence in Criminal Cases," [1963] Crim. L. Rev. 15, 77; R. S. O'Regan, "Admissibility of Confessions—The Standard of Proof," [1964] Crim. L. Rev. 287.

that English courts are little concerned with the way evidence was secured, as far as the issue of admissibility is concerned.

Where counsel for the defense intends to object to the admissibility of a confession, he is expected so to inform the prosecution beforehand, and it is considered good practice for the prosecution not to mention that piece of evidence in its opening statement to the jury.[50] The proper procedure, when the issue is raised, is for the judge first to hold a hearing on the question in the absence of the jury, but if he concludes that the confession is admissible, he must still tell the jury to reject it if they are not satisfied beyond reasonable doubt that it was voluntary.[51] If, however, the judge concludes that the confession is not voluntary, the evidence of the alleged confession should not be put before the jury.[52] Thus it is error for a judge to hold that the admissibility of a confession is solely a matter of law, and that the only issue is whether the statement was untrue.[53] Furthermore, the judge may not decide the question of the voluntariness of a confession merely by reference to depositions; the proper course is for the judge to hear evidence,[54] including the testimony of the accused.[55] When the issue goes to the jury, counsel for the accused is entitled to cross-examine the police and to try again to show that the confession had been obtained by means of a promise or favor, since "the weight and

50. R. v. Hammond (1941) 28 Cr. App. R. 84 (C.C.A.).

51. J. C. Smith, "Developments in the Law of Evidence, 1954–63," [1964] Crim. L. Rev. 434, 440. As to the necessity of a hearing in the United States, see Boles v. Stevenson, 379 U.S. 43 (1964).

52. R. v. Francis and Murphy (1959) 43 Cr. App. R. 174 (C.C.A.).

53. R. v. Parkinson, [1964] Crim. L. Rev. 398 (C.C.A.); R. v. Murray, [1951] 1 K.B. 391; R. v. Bass, [1953] 1 Q.B. 680.

54. R. v. Chadwick (1934) 24 Cr. App. R. 138 (C.C.A.).

55. R. v. Cowell (1940) 27 Cr. App. R. 191 (C.C.A.).

value of the evidence are always matters for the jury." [56] In this connection, the Court of Criminal Appeal has taken the position that in giving testimony before the judge, in the absence of the jury, it is not improper for the prosecution to ask the accused, on cross-examination, whether the confession was true, since it is a perfectly natural question that is relevant to the issue of coercion. [57]

The general rule is that a confession is not admissible if there had been fear of prejudice or hope of advantage held out by some person of authority. The term "person of authority" includes not only policemen but magistrates, jailers, prosecutors, prosecution solicitors, employers, magistrates' clerks, coroners, and warders. [58] Thus, a confession is admissible if it was induced by the promise of a person who does not in fact have any authority or power with respect to the prosecution. [59] But if such a person made the promise or inducement in the presence of a constable or other person with authority over the accused, then the effect is the same as if it were held out by one possessing the requisite authority. [60]

56. R. v. Murray, [1951] 1 K.B. 391, 34 Cr. App. R. 203 (C.C.A.), per Lord Goddard, C.J. See also R. v. O'Neill (1950) 34 Cr. App. R. 108 (C.C.A.); R. v. Sutherland and Johnson, [1959] Crim. L. Rev. 440 (C.C.A.)

57. R. v. Hammond (1941) 28 Cr. App. R. 84 (C.C.A.). See Rupert Cross, "The Function of the Judge and Jury with Regard to Confessions," [1960] Crim. L. Rev. 385.

58. For citations, see Stone's *Justices' Manual* (92nd ed. 1960), p. 352. See R. v. Swatkins (1831) 4 C. & P. 548, 172 E.R. 819 (N.P.).

59. R. v. Gibbons (1823) 1 C. & P. 97, 171 E.R. 1117 (N.P.); R. v. Tyler and Finch (1823) 1 C. & P. 129, 171 E.R. 1132 (N.P.); R. v. Frewin (1855) 6 Cox C.C. 530 (C.C.C.).

60. R. v. Pountney (1836) 7 C. & P. 302, 173 E.R. 134 (N.P.); R. v. Taylor (1839) 8 C. & P. 733, 173 E.R. 694 (N.P.); R. v. Laugher (1846) 2 Car. & Kirk. 225, 175 E.R. 93 (N.P.); R. v. Millen (1849) 3 Cox C.C. 507 (Kent Assizes).

Of course, it has long been the law in Britain that one may not be tortured into confessing to a crime,[61] but duress may take much more limited forms. Thus the police may not induce a confession through cross-examination of the accused,[62] although a confession is not improper if made voluntarily after a caution.[63] It is well established that where there has been no threat or inducement, one may voluntarily make admissions to a police officer before being taken into custody, and such admissions are later admissible as evidence.[64] Indeed, the fact that an accused person makes a voluntary confession without a caution does not mean that the confession must be excluded at the trial, even though there had been a technical violation of the Judges' Rules.[65] The controlling element is the absence of a threat or

61. Felton's Case (1628) 3 St. Tr. 367. The Court of Star Chamber was abolished by statute in 1641, 16 Car. 1, c. 10, and with it torture as a means of getting confessions disappeared. Though "third-degree" methods on the part of the police are rare, they are by no means unknown. For a recent incident see "Sheffield and Shawcross" (1963) 107 Sol. J. 877.

62. R. v. Matthews (1919) 14 Cr. App. R. 23 (C.C.A.); R. v. Brown and Bruce (1931) 23 Cr. App. R. 56 (C.C.A.); R. v. May (1952) 36 Cr. App. R. 91 (C.C.A.); R. v. Bass, [1953] 1 Q.B. 680, (1953) 37 Cr. App. R. 51 (C.C.A.); R. v. Godwin, [1924] 2 D.L.R. 362 (K.B.) (N.B.).

63. R. v. Hirst (1896) 18 Cox C.C. 374 (Manchester Assizes); R. v. James (1909) 2 Cr. App. R. 319 (C.C.A.); R. v. Unsworth (1910) 4 Cr. App. R. 1 (C.C.A.). See also R. v. Dingley (1845) 1 Car. & Kir. 637, 174 E.R. 970 (N.P.); R. v. Warren (1848) 11 L.T.O.S. 516, 12 J.P. 571 (C.C.); R. v. Baldry (1852) 2 Den, 430, 5 Cox C.C. 523 (C.C.R.); R. v. Gilhaus (1828) 1 Mood. 186, 168 E.R. 1235 (N.P.).

64. R. v. Miller (1895) 18 Cox C.C. 54 (Liverpool Assizes); R. v. Burgess, [1962] Crim. L. Rev. 469 (C.C.A.); R. v. Vernon (1872) 12 Cox C.C. 153 (Stafford Assizes); R. v. Thomas (1836) 7 C. & P. 345, 173 E.R. 154 (N.P.); R. v. Crowe and Myerscough (1917) 81 J.P. 288 (C.C.C.). See "Questioning an Accused Person" (1928) 92 J.P. 758.

65. R. v. Pattison (1929) 21 Cr. App. R. 139 (C.C.A.).

promise.[66] A mere statement by the employer of the accused, "Take care, Jarvis, we know more than you think we know," is neither a threat nor a promise of the kind that would render the reply inadmissible; it is only a warning or a bit of advice.[67] Similarly, where the police officer says in the course of the conversation, in asking questions before arrest, "I must know more about it," the court felt it would be straining the confessions rule "to an unnatural extent" to exclude on such a ground.[68] It has also been held that a confession induced merely by a hope of pardon formed in the prisoner's mind is admissible in evidence,[69] as is a statement made voluntarily to a fellow prisoner,[70] or in response to the spiritual admonitions of the prison chaplain.[71]

The law looks upon confessions with considerable suspicion; hence the rule that an uncorroborated confession is not generally regarded as sufficient to support a conviction.[72] Confessions induced by threats or bribes are excluded mainly because they are unreliable; if not necessarily false, they are at least suspect.[73] But in addition, the rule against coerced confessions is a sanction against the improper use of force by the police or by other persons endowed with authority. Lord Sumner once observed that coerced statements are rejected

66. R. v. Thornton (1824) 1 Mood 27, 168 E.R. 1171 (C.C.); R. v. Hawken (1898) 67 L.J.Q.B. 526, 19 Cox C.C. 122 (D.C.); R. v. Lambe (1791) 2 Leach 552, 168 E.R. 379 (C.C.).

67. R. v. Jarvis (1867) 10 Cox C.C. 574 (C.C.R.).

68. R. v. Reason (1872) 12 Cox C.C. 228 (Warwickshire Assizes)

69. R. v. Godinko (1911) 7 Cr. App. R. 12 (C.C.A.).

70. R. v. Shaw (1834) 6 C. & P. 372, 172 E.R. 1282 (N.P.).

71. R. v. Gilham (1828) 1 Mood. C.C. 186, 168 E.R. 1235 (C.C.R.). See also R. v Risborough (1847) 11 J.P. 280 (Norwich Assizes).

72. 2 Hale P.C. 225.

73. J. A. Andrews, "Involuntary Confessions and Illegally Obtained Evidence in Criminal Cases," [1963] Crim. L. Rev. 18.

mainly because of the danger to the due administration of justice.[74]

It is not surprising, therefore, that cases on this subject indicate that English judges are likely to have exacting standards on the issue of coercion.[75] It is wrong, for example, for a policeman to tell the accused to tell all he knows because "it will save trouble," for this is a most improper threat.[76] Similarly, it is not permissible for the interrogating policeman to say to the prisoner, "Why tell us a pack of lies? You had far better tell us the truth about the matter." [77] It is equally impermissible to induce a confession by telling the accused that it would or may be better for him to tell the truth and confess,[78] or to tell him that he must confess in order to avoid getting into trouble.[79] It is also improper to hold out such inducements as a promise of forgiveness by the employer,[80] a promise not to institute criminal proceedings,[81] a promise of lighter punishment,[82] or a promise of liberty.[83] It is improper for a committing

74. Ibrahim v. R., [1914] A.C. 599, 611 (P.C.).

75. See Z. Cowen and P. B. Carter, *Essays on the Law of Evidence* (Oxford: Clarendon Press, 1956), Chap. 3.

76. R. v. Cheverton (1862) 2 F. & F. 833, 175 E.R. 1308 (Chelmsford Assizes). For a list of expressions which led to the rejection of confessions, see Frank L. Bunn, *Evidence in Criminal Cases* (London: Street & Maxwell, 1957), p. 27.

77. R. v. Jones, [1955] Crim. L. Rev. 109 (Bedford. Q. Sess.).

78. R. v. Dunn (1831) 4 C. & P. 543, 172 E.R. 817 (N.P.); R. v. Fennell (1881) 7 Q.B.D. 147, 14 Cox C.C. 607 (C.C.R.); R. v. Hatts and Culffe (1883) 49 L.T. 780, 48 J.P. 248 (C.C.R.); R. v. Jones (1885) 49 J.P. 728 (Chester Assizes).

79. R. v. Coley (1868) 10 Cox C.C. 536 (C.C.C.).

80. R. v. Mansfield (1881) 14 Cox C.C. 639 (Derbyshire Assizes).

81. R. v. Barker, [1941] 2 K.B. 381, 29 Cr. App. R. 52 (C.C.A.); R. v. Boughton (1910) 6 Cr. App. R. 8 (C.C.A.).

82. R. v. Winsor (1864) 4 F. & F. 360, 176 E.R. 599 (N.P.).

83. R. v. Ackroyd (1824) 1 Lew. C.C. 49, 168 E.R. 954 (York Assizes).

magistrate to secure a confession by saying to the prisoner that, if he made the sought-for disclosure, the magistrate would do what he could for him.[84] Furthermore, English courts have rejected confessions on such grounds as a threat to call the police,[85] a threat of punishment,[86] or a threat to take the prisoner to a magistrate.[87] A court long ago ruled that it was improper for the police to get a confession by admonishing the prisoner not to add a lie to the crime he was accused of committing,[88] or by telling him that there are witnesses who will swear he committed the crime in question.[89]

The basic position of English law on confessions was well put in an 1893 decision of the High Court where a confession of embezzlement came as a result of a statement by the chairman of the company to the defendant's brother to the effect that it would be "the right thing . . . to make a clean breast of it."[90] The judge pointed out that to be admissible a confession must be free and voluntary. "If it proceeds from remorse and a desire to make reparation for the crime, it is admissible. If it flows from hope or fear, excited by a person in authority, it is inadmissible."[91] Furthermore, the prosecution must prove affirmatively that the confession was free and voluntary. Here, the court held, the communication was calculated to lead the prisoner

84. R. v. Cooper (1833) 5 C. & P. 535, 172 E.R. 1087 (N.P.). Cf. R. v. Partridge (1836) 7 C. & P. 551, 173 E.R. 243 (N.P.).

85. R. v. Hearn (1841) 1 Car. & M. 109, 174 E.R. 431 (N.P.).

86. R. v. Parratt (1831) 4 C. & P. 570, 172 E.R. 825 (N.P.).

87. R. v. Thompson (1783) 1 Leach 291, 168 ER. 248 (C.C.).

88. R. v. Shepard (1836) 7 C. & P. 579, 173 E.R. 255 (N.P.). Cf. R. v. Morton (1843) 2 Mood & R. 514, 174 E.R. 367 (N.P.).

89. R. v. Mills (1833) 6 C. & P. 146, 172 E.R. 1183 (N.P.). Cf. R. v. Rue (1876) 34 L.T. 400, 13 Cox C.C. 209 (Somerset Assizes).

90. R. v. Thompson, [1893] 2 Q.B. 12 (C.C.R.) (Cave, J.).

91. *Id.* at 15.

to believe that it would be better for himself to say *something*. Said the judge: "I always suspect these confessions, which are supposed to be the offspring of penitence and remorse, and which nevertheless are repudiated by the prisoner at the trial. It is remarkable that it is of very rare occurrence for evidence of a confession to be given when the proof of the prisoner's guilt is otherwise clear and satisfactory; but, when it is not clear and satisfactory, the prisoner is not infrequently alleged to have been seized with the desire born of penitence and remorse to supplement it with a confession;—a desire which vanishes as soon as he appears in a court of justice." [92]

Searches and Seizures

Though the common law of England gradually adopted a position of opposition to the use of general search warrants, in the sixteenth and seventeenth centuries the government often utilized such warrants through the prerogative courts of Star Chamber and High Commission. The government was concerned mainly with sedition, particularly with actions for seditious libel against authors and printers, though it also resorted to general warrants in respect to tax collections, trade regulation, and the customs service. Since the authorities did not always know what would turn up—for example, in searching for stolen goods—they could not be specific. In a series of notable cases decided in 1763–65, the courts outlawed the use of general warrants, and since that time this instrumentality of oppression has been regarded as illegal. When the secretary of state issued a general warrant to search for the authors, printers, and publishers of the anonymously

92. *Id.*

published *North Briton* pamphlets, which sharply criticized the government of the day, John Wilkes defied
the warrant as "a ridiculous warrant against the whole
English nation" and, after his imprisonment, won a substantial verdict in Lord Camden's court for false imprisonment.[93]

In one case [94] the court ruled that a general warrant
to arrest unnamed persons, where no charges had yet
been stated, was unlawful. In another case [95] the court
ruled that it was illegal to seize the papers of an unnamed person on a general warrant. In the leading case
of *Entick* v. *Carrington*,[96] Lord Camden not only condemned the general character of the warrants in question but went on to point out that they had been issued
to search for evidence, thus connecting the rule against
unreasonable searches with the privilege against self-
incrimination. "It is very certain," he declared, "that
the law obligeth no man to accuse himself; because the
necessary means of compelling self accusation, falling
upon the innocent as well as the guilty, would be both
cruel and unjust, and it would seem, that search for
evidence is disallowed upon the same principle." Thus
Lord Camden held that general warrants were unlawful because they were uncertain, and that the search
for evidence violates the privilege against self-incrimination. "By the laws of England," he declared, "every
invasion of private property, be it ever so minute, is a
trespass," and he could find no statute or rule of com-

93. See George Rudé, *Wilkes and Liberty* (Oxford: Clarendon
Press, 1962).
94. Leach v. Money (1765) 19 St. Tr. 1002.
95. Wilkes v. Wood (1763) 19 St. Tr. 1154.
96. (1765) 19 St. Tr. 1029, K. & L. 174. See E. C. S. Wade and
G. G. Phillips, *Constitutional Law* (6th ed.; London: Longmans,
Green, 1960), pp. 468–70.

mon law which justified this invasion. As for the argument of state necessity, Lord Camden said that he could make no distinction between state offenses and other offenses, declaring that "the common law does not understand that kind of reasoning, nor do our books take note of any such distinctions."

At the common law there is no power to issue a warrant for the search of a house except in the case of stolen goods.[97] But many statutes permit the search of houses for various specific purposes. Thus the Forgery Act, 1913, section 16, provides that a justice may grant a search warrant "if it shall be made to appear by information on oath before a justice of the peace that

97. Entick v. Carrington (1765) 19 St. Tr. 1029, 1067. See Larceny Act, 1916, s. 42. On the basis of information given on oath, if a justice thinks that there is reasonable cause to believe that an individual has in his possession or on his premises any property with respect to which an offense against the act has been committed, he may grant a warrant to search. In addition, under certain circumstances a chief police office may authorize a constable, in writing, to enter and search premises for any property believed to be stolen. See Jones v. German, [1897] 1 Q.B. 374 (C.A.), which held that a search warrant may be issued on an allegation of reasonable suspicion of larceny; it is not necessary to allege that a larceny has in fact been committed. A similar holding was made in Willey v. Peace, [1951] 1 K.B. 94. Whether there was reasonable suspicion, Lord Hewart ruled in Ludlow v. Skelton, *The Times,* Feb. 3 and 4, 1938, is a question for the judge, and not the jury, to decide, and he held that a constable who has no reasonable suspicion before his suspect refuses to answer questions cannot assert that his suspicion becomes reasonable merely because of that refusal. Said Lord Hewart, "It is a perilous thing when great powers, with the knowledge of great force behind, are recklessly, foolishly, or over-zealously applied. If once one ceases in this country to value the liberty of the subject, if once signs are shown of giving way to the abominable doctrine that, because things are done by officials, therefore some immunity must be extended to them, what is to become of liberty?" Lord Hewart had a penchant for hyperbole: see Lord Gordon H. Hewart, *The New Despotism* (London: Benn, 1929). The earliest statute authorizing search for stolen goods was the Metropolitan Police Act, 1839, s. 66.

there is reasonable cause to believe" that an individual has in his possession forged bank notes, or any forged document, or equipment to make the same. The Coinage Offences Act, 1936, section 11, authorizes search for counterfeit coins and tools of the counterfeiting trade. The Children and Young Persons Act, 1933, section 40, authorizes search for ill-treated or neglected children. Under the Obscene Publications Act, 1857, section 1, and the Obscene Publications Act, 1959, section 3, the police may search for obscene books and pictures, and under the Criminal Libel Act, 1819, section 1, for obscene libels. Searches are also authorized by the Official Secrets Act, 1911, section 9, and the Official Secrets Act, 1920, section 11, for sketches, plans, and documents which fall within their ambit. Many other statutes authorize searches.[98] Speaking generally, the police have the statutory right to enter and inspect some types of businesses, such as those dealing with liquor, explosives, or certain drugs, or those that are required to keep records, such as dealers in scrap metal or poisons.[99] In addition, some local acts give special powers of entry and inspection in respect to the premises of clubs, theatrical agencies, and brokers in certain trades.[100] Some statutes authorize the issuance of war-

---

98. See also Canals (Offences) Act, 1840, s. 11; Poaching Prevention Act, 1862, s. 2; Public Stores Act, 1875, s. 6; Merchandise Marks Act, 1887, s. 12; Port of London Authority Act, 1917; Incitement to Disaffection Act, 1934, s. 2 (2); Public Order Act, 1936, s. 2; Firearms Act, 1937, s. 26; Sexual Offences Act, 1956, s. 43. See Glanville Williams, "Statutory Powers of Search and Arrest on the Ground of Unlawful Possession," [1960] Crim. L. Rev. 598–610. In all, there are about seventy statutes that authorize search warrants in respect to certain offenses.

99. Report of the Royal Commission on Police Powers and Procedures, 1929, Cmd. 3297, para. 34.

100. *Ibid.* See, e.g., Licensing Act, 1953.

rants if there is reasonable ground to believe that a breach of the law has taken place; others permit warrants where there is reason to suspect that an offense has occurred.

Speaking generally, the police have a right to search any person who has been lawfully arrested. This right is based partly on the right of the police to protect themselves and make an effective arrest, and partly on their duty to discover and preserve evidence.[101] Furthermore, as a Royal Commission observed in 1929, "it has long been the practice of the Police to search the dwelling of a person for whose arrest a warrant has been issued, and, in cases of arrest without warrant, to search premises as well as the arrested person, in cases of serious crime whenever it seems likely that any material evidence can be obtained. In normal cases, the Police obtain the consent of the occupiers before carrying out a search in such circumstances. But it appears that, in the event of a refusal to consent, the Police, if they proceed with the search, may be faced with the risk of a subsequent action for trespass. This is a risk which is commonly taken by the Police and the practice seems to have had the tacit approval of the Courts

101. See Bessell v. Wilson (1853) 20 L.T. O.S. 233, 1 E. & B. 489, 492 (Q.B.); Leigh v. Cole (1853) 6 Cox C.C. 329 (Staffordshire Assizes). See Report of the Royal Commission on Police Powers and Procedures, 1929, Cmd. 3297, para. 32: "We understand that there is no express power to search the person even of arrested prisoners, but it has long been the practice of the Police to search persons who are taken into custody for any serious offence. This is a necessary and obvious precaution, not merely to obtain possible evidence bearing on the charge but to deprive the arrested person of any means of injuring himself or others whilst he is in custody." See also Sargent v. West, [1964] Crim. L. Rev. 412 (Q.B.D.), which held that a policeman in London may search a person if there is a reasonable suspicion that he has property on his person that had been stolen or obtained unlawfully.

for so long that, in the opinion of the Home Office, it has become part of the common law." [102]

Indeed, the High Court went even further in 1934, in *Elias* v. *Pasmore*,[103] when it ruled that where the police have lawfully arrested a person, under the authority of a search warrant, they may not only search the premises and seize documents belonging to that person, but they may also seize documents belonging to others, provided that the documents might properly be used in a prosecution of someone for some crime. This rule, which was justified in the interests of the state, has been severely criticized as being wholly unwarranted by law,[104] and it is not entirely clear that it is followed today.

Since the English courts do not follow the American exclusionary rule, evidence secured unlawfully is fully

102. Report of the Royal Commission on Police Powers and Procedures, 1929, Cmd. 3297, para. 33. See Davis v. Lisle, [1936] 2 K.B. 434, which held that where a constable enters a property without a search warrant and without the permission of the owner, he is a mere trespasser from the moment the owner has ordered him to leave, even though the original entry to make inquiry may have been legal. On American law see E. W. Machen, Jr., *The Law of Search and Seizure* (Chapel Hill: Institute of Government, University of North Carolina, 1950).

103. [1934] 2 K.B. 164, 50 T.L.R. 196.

104. See E. C. S. Wade, "Police Search" (1934) 50 L.Q. Rev. 354, 359: "How can the public enjoy the protection to liberty of person and property secured by the General Warrant Cases if the existence of a warrant for the arrest of A enables the police to hunt for information throughout the building where A happens to be at the time of his arrest and use material thus discovered to prosecute, say, D, who alone out of B, C, D, E, and F is thus shown to have committed a crime? Is not D, as well as B, C, E and F, presumed to be innocent and immune from invasion of his private property by the police, unless and until charged with an offence connected therewith, or in the case of the statutory exceptions reasonably suspected of the commission of, such an offence?"

admissible. As Lord Goddard, the Lord Chief Justice, said in 1955, "the test to be applied in considering whether evidence is admissible is whether it is relevant to the matters at issue. If it is, it is admissible and the court is not concerned with how the evidence was obtained." [105] Thus, if it is true that the exclusionary rule exerts a deterrent influence on the police in America, then this rule is absent in Britain. Whether the common law rule on the admissibility of evidence wrongfully secured has encouraged police lawlessness in this area is almost impossible to determine. Certainly the English police do not have a reputation for lawlessness in respect to searches and seizures.

It remains to be noted that the government has long had the power to intercept communications, including the power to wiretap. The power to intercept communications is very ancient and has been recognized by many statutes covering the last two or more centuries. The power is used to prevent and detect serious crimes and to preserve the safety of the state, and it is utilized almost exclusively by the Metropolitan Police, the Board of Customs and Excise, and the Security Service. A special committee of privy councillors reported in 1957 that this power was used "with the greatest care and circumspection, under the strictest rules and safeguards," and never without the personal approval of the Home Secretary.[106] The Home Secretary must be satisfied that it would be in the public interest to grant a warrant, and he observes the following conditions: (1) the offense must be really serious; (2) normal

105. Kuruma, Son of Kaniu v. Reginam, [1955] A.C. 197 (P.C.).
106. Report of the Committee of Privy Councillors Appointed to Inquire into the Interception of Communications, October, 1957, Cmd. 283, p. 6.

methods of investigation must have been tried and found wanting; and (3) there must be good reason to think that interception will result in a conviction.[107] It was noted that warrants for interception are granted very sparingly. For example, in 1956, only 183 letter and 159 telephone interceptions were authorized. The special committee concluded that the practice should be allowed to continue. It said that "the interference with the privacy of the ordinary law-abiding citizen or with his individual liberty is infinitesimal, and only arises as an inevitable incident of intercepting the communications of some wrongdoer. It has produced no harmful consequences." [108]

Use of Wrongfully Secured Evidence

English courts are not obliged to exclude evidence merely because it was procured wrongly, by a tort or by a crime.[109] The Privy Council recently pointed out in a leading case that the test of the admissibility of evidence is whether it is relevant to the matters in issue.[110] As Lord Goddard had said, if it is admissible then the court is not concerned with how the evidence was obtained. At the same time it was pointed out that the judge always has discretion to disallow evidence that will operate unfairly against an accused person.[111] The rule that confessions must be voluntary

107. *Ibid.*, p. 17
108. *Ibid.*, p. 6.
109. R. v. Gould (1840) 9 C. & P. 364, 173 E.R. 870 (N.P.); Lloyd v. Mostyn (1842) 10 M. & W. 478, 12 L.J. Exch. 1, 152 E.R. 558; Calcraft v. Guest, [1898] 1 Q.B. 759; Ashburton v. Pape, [1913] 2 Ch. 649.
110. Kuruma v. R., [1955] A.C. 197 (P.C.).
111. Kuruma v. R., [1955] A.C. 197, 204 (P.C.); Noor Mohamed v. R., [1949] A.C. 182, 192 (P.C.); Harris v. D.P.P., [1952] A.C. 694, 707 (H.L.); R. v. Cook, [1959] 2 Q.B. 340 (C.C.A.); R. v. Flynn,

to be admissible is an exception to the general proposition that wrongfully secured evidence may be used. But it has been held that even if a confession is obtained in such a manner as to be inadmissible in evidence, if in the course of that confession a clue is given to other evidence which will prove the case, the latter evidence is admissible.[112] The rule on confessions also applies to documents: if, as a result of a promise, inducement, or threat, documents are produced by the person to whom the promise or inducement is held out or the threat made, then the documents stand on precisely the same footing as an oral or a written confession that is brought into existence as a result of such a promise, inducement, or threat.[113]

While the rule concerning the admissibility of wrongfully secured evidence is well established, it has nevertheless often been criticized.[114] Of course the admission of such evidence does not mean that the trial judge is condoning the illegality; he is saying, in effect, that it is a matter for a later and separate action. At the same time, it is worth noting that there seem to be very few cases in which the issue arises. This may well be the

[1961] 3 All E.R. 58, [1961] 3 W.L.R. 907 (C.C.A.); Callis v. Gunn (1963) 107 S.J. 831 (Q.B.D.).

112. R. v. Leatham (1861) 3 E. & E. 658, 8 Cox C.C. 498 (Q.B.).

113. R. v. Barker, [1941] 2 K.B. 381. As to what constitutes an improper inducement see R. v. Nowell, [1948] 2 All E.R. 794 (C.C.A.).

114. See Cowen and Carter, *Essays on the Law of Evidence*, p. 72; Glanville Williams, "Evidence Obtained by Illegal Means," [1955] Crim. L. Rev. 339; J. A. Andrews, "Involuntary Confession and Illegally Obtained Evidence in Criminal Cases," [1963] Crim. L. Rev. 15–20, 77–83. American law on this subject runs the other way. In Weeks v. United States, 232 U.S. 383 (1914), the U.S. Supreme Court held that evidence secured unlawfully was excludable on pretrial motion in federal courts, and in Mapp v. Ohio, 367 U.S. 643 (1961), the court applied the federal exclusionary rule to the states as a requirement of due process of law.

result of good police work, but it may also be that the rule on admissibility is so well established, or the point so difficult to prove, that counsel do not raise the issue.

Habeas Corpus

As in the United States, the writ of habeas corpus offers persons charged with a crime one of their most important protections against injustice. Hallam declared that the writ "is the principal bulwark of English liberty. . . ." [115] Lord Halsbury once said that "for a period extending as far back as our legal history, the writ of habeas corpus has been regarded as one of the most important safeguards of the liberty of the subject." [116] Furthermore, the writ loses none of its significance because it is wholly procedural in character. As Dicey pointed out, "the Habeas Corpus Acts declare no principles and define no rights, but they are for practical purposes worth a hundred constitutional articles guaranteeing individual liberty." [117] The central importance

115. Henry Hallam, *View of the State of Europe during the Middle Ages* (New York: Middleton, 1872), II, 310. See also Wade and Phillips, *Constitutional Law*, pp. 473–82.

116. Cox v. Hakes (1890) 15 App. Cas. 506, 514 (H.L.). Cf. the remarks of the Earl of Birkenhead in Home Secretary v. O'Brien, [1923] A.C. 603, 609 (H.L.): "We are dealing with a writ antecedent to statute, and throwing its root deep into the genius of our common law. . . . It is perhaps the most important writ known to the constitutional law of England, affording as it does a swift and imperative remedy in all cases of illegal restraint or confinement. It is of immemorial antiquity. . . . It has through the ages been jealously maintained by Courts of Law as a check upon the illegal usurpation of power by the Executive at the cost of the liege."

117. A. V. Dicey, *Introduction to the Study of the Law of the Constitution*, E. C. S. Wade, ed. (10th ed.; London and New York: Macmillan, 1959), p. 199. Cf. Lord Shaw of Dunfermline in R. v. Halliday, [1917] A.C. 260, 294 (H.L.) (dissenting): "The Habeas Corpus Acts are, it is true, procedure Acts. In one sense they confer no rights upon the subject, but they provide a means whereby his fundamental rights

of the writ is reflected in the fact that an application for habeas corpus takes precedence over all other business in English courts.[118]

The writ is, of course, available for judicial inquiry into the legality of any confinement in a penal institution or police station, but it also extends to any other form of restraint upon personal liberty.[119] Thus, the writ of habeas corpus has been used to free slaves,[120] to challenge extradition proceedings,[121] to test imprisonment by order of the House of Commons,[122] to free a wife from restraint by her husband,[123] to free a person from an institution for mental defectives,[124] to take a child from the control of foster parents,[125] and to test the legality of detention by military authorities.[126] The

shall be vindicated, his freedom from arrest except on justifiable legal process shall be secured, and arbitrary attack upon liberty and life shall be promptly and effectually foiled by law."

118. Lord Shaw of Dunfermline once said, Home Secretary v. O'Brien, [1923] A.C. 603, 643 (H.L.): "urgency is written all over the face of habeas corpus proceedings. 'Preventing delay,' 'immediate determination of the right to the applicant's freedom,' the avoidance of 'the delay and uncertainty of ordinary litigation'—these expressions are significant of urgency as an essential quality of the proceedings."

119. Application of the writ to persons deprived of their liberty for reasons other than a criminal charge was first authorized by the Habeas Corpus Act, 1816.

120. Sommersett's Case (1772) 20 St. Tr. 1.

121. De Demko v. Home Secretary, [1959] A.C. 654 (H.L.); R. v. Governor of Brixton Prison, *Ex parte* Shuter, [1960] 2 Q.B. 89; R. v. Governor of Brixton Prison, *Ex parte* Kolczynski, [1955] 1 Q.B. 540; *In re* Castioni, [1891] 1 Q.B. 149.

122. The Case of the Sheriff of Middlesex (1840) 11 A. & E. 273, 113 E.R. 419 (K.B.).

123. R. v. Jackson, [1891] 1 Q.B. 671. See also Barnardo v. Ford, [1892] A.C. 326 (H.L.).

124. R. v. Board of Control, *Ex parte* Rutty, [1956] 2 Q.B. 109.

125. *In re* A.B., [1954] 2 Q.B. 385. See also Barnardo v. McHugh, [1891] A.C. 388 (H.L.).

126. Case of Wolf Tone (1798) 27 St. Tr. 614; R. v. Governor of Wormwood Scrubs Prison, *Ex parte* Boydell, [1948] 2 K.B. 193.

writ is in fact available to all persons in Britain with
the exception of enemy prisoners of war and interned
enemy aliens.[127] Since the claim to personal liberty is
of crucial importance, where the prisoner is himself unable to apply for the writ, it may be sought in his behalf
by someone else.[128]

At the common law, denial by a judge or court of an
application for habeas corpus was not regarded as *res
judicata,* and therefore the request could go from judge
to judge or court to court in successive applications.[129]
Thus the House of Lords said in 1890, "A person detained in custody might thus proceed from court to
court until he obtained his liberty." [130] Lord Goddard
once explained that the reason for this rule was not the
Stuart judges' love of liberty, but the technical fact that
where a court or judge merely refused to grant the
writ, there was no judgment in a formal sense.[131] While
there were holdings to the effect that an applicant
could make successive applications from court to

127. See R. v. Vine Street Police Superintendent, *Ex parte* Lieb-
mann, [1916] 1 K.B. 268; R. v. Halliday, [1017] A.C. 200 (H.L.). Cf.
Greene v. Secretary of State for Home Affairs, [1942] A.C. 284 (H.L.).
It has been argued that the Emergency Powers Act, 1939, which gave
the executive the power of detention without trial, did not suspend the
writ of habeas corpus, which was still available, but merely widened
the area of lawful detention. R. F. V. Heuston, *Essays in Constitutional
Law* (London: Stevens, 1961), p. 104.

128. Habeas Corpus Act, 1679, s. 2; Cobbett v. Hudson (1850) 15
Q.B. 988; *Ex parte* Child (1854) 15 C.B. 238, 139 E.R. 413 (C.P.);
Re Thompson (1860) 30 L.J.M.C. 19, 9 Cox C.C. 70 (Ex.).

129. King v. Suddis (1801) 1 East 306, 102 E.R. 119 (K.B.); Bur-
dett v. Abbot (1811) 14 East 1, 90, 104 E.R. 501, 535 (K.B.); *Ex
parte* Partington (1845) 13 M. & W. 679, 153 E.R. 284 (Ex.). See
William S. Church, *A Treatise on the Writ of Habeas Corpus* (San
Francisco: Bancroft-Whitney Co., 1893), sec. 386.

130. Cox v. Hakes, [1890] A.C. 506, 527 (H.L.) (Lord Herschell).

131. Lord Goddard, C.J., "A Note on Habeas Corpus" (1949) 65
L.Q. Rev. 30–36.

court,[132] or even from judge to judge of the same court,[133] Lord Parker, the Lord Chief Justice, ruled in 1959 that an applicant for a writ of habeas corpus in a criminal cause who had once been heard by a divisional court of the Queen's Bench Division cannot be heard again, on a renewed application based on the same evidence and the same grounds, by another divisional court of the same division, since under the Judicature Act of 1873 the divisional courts exercise all or any part of the jurisdiction of the High Court.[134] A decision of the divisional court is thus equivalent to the decision of all the judges of the Queen's Bench Division. Prior to 1873 there were three separate law courts—King's Bench, Common Pleas, and Exchequer—and since each sat *en banc,* no individual judge had any power to act for the court. Thus, while the applicant for the writ could undoubtedly go from court to court, Lord Parker noted that he could not apply twice to the same court on the same facts.[135] While the decision not to grant the writ is not a judgment, so that there is no *res judicata,* an exercise of judicial discretion is involved. "The court must have an inherent jurisdiction," Lord Parker said, "to refuse, having once exercised its discretion, to hear the same matter argued again." [136] Since a divisional court of Queen's Bench, sitting to hear applications for habeas corpus, is the successor of the three common law courts sitting *en banc,* its decision is

132. Eshugbayai Eleko v. Government of Nigeria, [1928] A.C. 459, 468 (P.C.).

133. Lord Halsbury, L.C., in Cox v. Hakes (1890) 15 App. Cas. 506, 514 (H.L.); Denning, L.J., in *Ex parte* Chapple (1950) 66 T.L.R. (Pt. 2) 932, 936 (C.A.).

134. *Re* Hastings, [1959] 1 Q.B. 358.

135. See Heuston, *Essays in Constitutional Law,* pp. 109–21.

136. *Re* Hastings, [1959] 1 Q.B. 358, 371.

equivalent to the decision of all the judges of the division.

The matter of successive applications for habeas corpus is now controlled by section 14 (2) of the Administration of Justice Act, 1960, which provides as follows: "Notwithstanding anything in any enactment or rule of law, where a criminal or civil application for habeas corpus has been made by or in respect of any person, no such application shall again be made by or in respect of that person on the same grounds, whether to the same court or judge or to any other court or judge, unless fresh evidence is adduced in support of the application; and no such application shall in any case be made to the Lord Chancellor." Thus Parliament has settled the matter by forbidding successive identical applications for the writ.

In the past, there was no appeal to a higher court from a decision to grant the writ of habeas corpus,[137] since such a decision was not an acquittal;[138] but one who failed to get the writ could appeal from court to court until he reached the highest available court.[139] However, under the Administration of Justice Act, 1960, section 1, either side in a habeas corpus proceeding now has the right of appeal, and under section 15 (3) of the act it is not necessary for the divisional court or the House of Lords, when granting the appeal, to certify

137. Cox v. Hakes (1890) 15 App. Cas. 506 (H.L.).

138. Lord Goddard took the view that the real reason for this rule was that there never was any method of appeal from the judgment of a superior court except by error, and error did not lie in the case of a prerogative writ. "A Note on Habeas Corpus" (1949) 65 L.Q. Rev. 30.

139. Home Secretary v. O'Brien, [1923] A.C. 603, 610 (H.L.) (Lord Birkenhead, L.C.). No appeal lies to the Court of Criminal Appeal from a decision to grant or refuse a writ of habeas corpus, because there has been no sentence or conviction to appeal from.

expressly that the case involves a point of law of general public importance. In a criminal proceeding a single judge cannot deny an application for the writ of habeas corpus but must refer it to the divisional court.[140] In criminal cases, appeal lies to the House of Lords directly from the divisional court; only in civil cases does appeal lie through the Court of Appeal.[141]

140. In *Ex parte* Mwenya, [1959] 3 W.L.R. 767, [1959] All E.R. 525, the Court of Appeals ruled that the divisional court of Queen's Bench had jurisdiction to issue the writ to a custodian in the protectorate of Northern Rhodesia, on the ground that jurisdiction extends to all territories "under the subjection of the Crown," whatever their labels. The test is not whether there has been formal annexation, but rather "the propriety and effectiveness of issuing it." (Romer, L.J.) The issue is whether the court to which application for the writ is made can make an order that can be enforced. (Sellers, L.J.) See Note, 23 Mod. Law Rev. 73–77 (1960).

141. See *Ex parte* Amand, [1943] A.C. 147 (H.L.). Under the Supreme Court of Judicature (Consolidation) Act, 1925, s. 31 (1), no appeal lies to the Court of Appeals "from any judgment of the High Court in any criminal cause or matter." See also King v. Governor of Brixton Prison, *Ex parte* Savarkar, [1910] 2 K.B. 1056 (C.A.).

IV

The Right to a Fair Trial

Some Elements of a Fair Trial

THE idea of a fair trial is an essential part of the English lawyer's concept of justice,[1] and there is wide agreement in England as to what constitutes the elements of a fair trial. Lord Hewart, C.J., once said that a fair trial comes to this: the parties are treated as equals before the court; they are heard in public; the judge is identified and is personally responsible for his decision; and there is a right of appeal on questions of procedure.[2] More recently, Lord Denning stated that the basic principles of justice are as follows: judges must be "absolutely independent of the Government"; the judge must be impartial and have no interest in any matter he tries, since no man can be judge in his own cause; before deciding against a party the judge must consider all he has to say, since no one should be con-

1. F. E. Dowrick, *Justice According to the English Common Lawyers* (London: Butterworth, 1961), Chap. 3.
2. Gordon H. Hewart, *The New Despotism* (London: Benn, 1929), pp. 9–164.

demned unheard; the judge must act only on the evidence and arguments properly before him; the judge must give reasons for his decision; the judge's own character should be beyond reproach; and each party should be free to state its case as strongly as it can.[3]

These basic ingredients of a fair trial are well established in English court decisions. It is perfectly clear that the accused has a right to be present in court throughout his trial,[4] although there is some authority for the proposition that the defendant may be excluded from the courtroom, and the trial may go on without him, if he persistently creates disturbance and disrupts the trial.[5] Furthermore, it is possible for one who is charged with a summary offense to plead guilty without appearing in magistrates' court,[6] but the court may not sentence an accused person to prison or subject him to any disqualification without his being there.[7]

The accused is entitled to know just what offense he is charged with, and an indictment is defective if it does not clearly state the nature of the offense charged.[8] Furthermore, as Lord Herschell, the Lord Chancellor, once wrote: "It is undoubtedly not competent for the prosecution to adduce evidence tending to show that the accused has been guilty of criminal acts other than

3. Sir Alfred Denning, *The Road to Justice* (London: Stevens, 1955), pp. 1–44.

4. R. v. St. George (1840) 9 C. & P. 483, 173 E.R. 921 (N.P.); R. v. Hales, [1924] 1 K.B. 602 (C.C.A.).

5. R. v. Berry (1897) 104 L.T.J. 110 (Northampton Assizes); R. v. Browne (1906) 70 J.P. 472 (C.C.C.). See Daniel E. Murray, "The Power to Expel a Criminal Defendant from his Own Trial: A Comparative View," 36 U. Colo. L. Rev. 171–86 (1964).

6. Magistrates' Court Act, 1957, s. 1.

7. *Ibid.*, s. (2) (iii), applied in R. v. Totton Justices, *The Times*, June 4, 1958 (Q.B.D.), where a three-months disqualification of a speeder was set aside.

8. R. v. McVitie, [1960] 2 Q.B. 483 (C.C.A.); R. v. Yule, [1964] 1 Q.B. (C.C.A.).

those covered by the indictment, for the purpose of leading to the conclusion that the accused is a person likely from his criminal conduct or character to have committed the offence for which he is being tried." [9]

There must be evidence to support a conviction for a crime, and the Court of Criminal Appeal will quash a conviction where there is no evidence at all that the defendant committed any crime. [10] Furthermore, the accused has a right to cross-examine anyone who gives evidence against him; thus, where a codefendant gives evidence against the accused, the judge has no discretion to disallow the cross-examination. [11] In the interests of justice, the prosecution is not free to withhold from the jury any evidence bearing on the case. It has been asserted that "it has been the duty of the Crown from time immemorial, and assuredly will remain so so long as our legal system endures, that the prosecution will lay before the jury for their consideration all the material evidence at their disposal. It is not for the prosecution to pick and choose." [12] Indeed, the prosecution must disclose all of their evidence to the accused before he is tried on an indictment; the element of surprise is ruled out entirely.

The idea of a fair trial in English law also embodies

9. Makin v. A.G. for New South Wales, [1894] A.C. 57, 65 (P.C.).

10. R. v. White (1918) 13 Cr. App. R. 211 (C.C.A.). See also R. v. George (1703) 6 Mod. Rep. 57, 87 E.R. 818 (K.B.): "A person cannot be convicted without proof." The U.S. Supreme Court has ruled that such a conviction violates due process: Thompson v. Louisville, 362 U.S. 199 (1960); Garner v. Louisiana, 368 U.S. 157 (1961).

11. R. v. McGuirk (1903) 107 S.J. 912 (C.C.A.). The U.S. Supreme Court took a similar position in Douglas v. Alabama, 380 U.S. 415 (1965).

12. R. v. McNally, *Daily Telegraph,* Feb. 28, 1962 (Bedford. Q. Sess.). In a prosecution for drunken driving the prosecutor failed to call as a witness a doctor who had examined the accused. The Recorder held that no one had a right to decide that the court and jury should not have the benefit of hearing the doctor's opinion.

the concept of an impartial, disinterested judge. The High Court once ruled that it was highly improper for an acting clerk of the justices, who was at the same time a member of a firm of solicitors representing one of the parties in a pending civil action for damages, to retire with the justices when they considered their decision, even though the justices stated on affidavit later on that the clerk had not in fact been consulted.[13] Said Lord Hewart, the Chief Justice: "it is not merely of some importance but is of fundamental importance that justice should not only be done, but should manifestly and undoubtedly be seen to be done. The question therefore is not whether in this case the deputy clerk made any observation or offered any criticism which he might not properly have made or offered; the question is whether he was so related to the case in its civil aspect as to be unfit to act as clerk to the justices in the criminal matter. The answer to that question depends not upon what actually was done but upon what might appear to be done. Nothing is to be done which creates even a suspicion that there has been an improper interference with the course of justice."

Finally, English law is much more strict than American law in forbidding newspaper comment on cases that are still *sub judice,* and the rules on this subject are very old and well established.[14] Thus Lord Hardwicke, the Lord Chancellor, said in 1742 that there was nothing "of more pernicious consequence, than to prejudice the minds of the public against persons concerned

13. R. v. Sussex Justices, [1924] 1 K.B. 256. For an application of the same rule in a civil action, see R. v. Essex Justices, [1927] 2 K.B. 475.

14. See A. L. Goodhart, "Newspapers and Contempt of Court in English Law," 48 Harv. L. Rev. 885 (1935).

as parties in causes, before the cause is finally heard." [15]
He went on to say: "It is a contempt of court, to prejudice mankind against persons before the case is heard.
There cannot be anything of greater consequence, than
to keep the streams of justice clear and pure, that parties
may proceed with safety both to themselves and to
their characters." That English courts will not permit
trial by newspaper is evidenced by the many contempt
proceedings brought against newspapers.[16] English law,
however, does permit the publication of pretrial evidence, and the widest sort of publicity is actually given
by the newspapers to the pretrial testimony of the
prosecution witnesses alone. This practice nullifies to
some extent the protection that the general rule extends
to persons accused of crime.[17]

Public Trial

In accord with Bentham's dictum that publicity is
essential to justice,[18] English criminal law procedure is
committed to the principle of the public trial. Thus a

15. Roach v. Garvan (1742) 2 Atk. 469, 26 E.R. 683 (Ch.).

16. For recent cases see: R. v. *Evening Standard* (1924) 40 T.L.R.
833 (K.B.); R. v. *Daily Mirror,* [1927] 1 K.B. 845; R. v. Bolam, *Ex
parte* Haigh (1949) 93 S.J. 220 (K.B.D.); R. v. *Evening Standard,*
[1954] 1 All E.R. 1026 (Q.B.); R. v. Odhams Press, Ltd., [1957] 1
Q.B. 73; R. v. Griffiths, [1957] 2 Q.B. 192. See Note, "Free Speech
vs. the Fair Trial in English and American Law of Contempt by Publication," 17 U. Chi. L. Rev. 540 (1950); Justice, *Contempt of Court*
(London: Stevens, 1959), pp. 8–16.

17. For an account of the extensive publicity given by the newspapers to the testimony at the preliminary hearing of a famous recent
murder case, see Louis Blom-Cooper, *The A6 Murder: Regina v. James
Hanratty* (London: Penguin Books, 1963). The Scottish rule is otherwise, for Scottish law will not permit much pretrial publicity. Mc-
Lauchlan v. Carson (1826) 6 S. 135; Smith v. Ritchie (1892) 20 R.
(J.) 52; MacAlister v. Assoc. Newspapers, [1954] Scots L.T.R. 14.

18. See Jeremy Bentham, *Rationale of Judicial Evidence* (London:
Hunt & Clarke, 1827), I, 511–606.

recent statute states that, except as otherwise provided by law, all magistrates shall sit in open court.[19] Similarly, the concept of the public trial is deeply rooted in English case law. In 1829 a High Court decision emphasized that in a summary judicial proceeding in a Court of Petty Sessions the magistrate may not, without any specific reason, remove from the courtroom a party who claimed a right to be present.[20] The court said that "it is one of the essential qualities of a Court of Justice that its proceedings should be public, and that all parties who may be desirous of hearing what is going on, if there be room in the place for that purpose,—provided they do not interrupt the proceedings, and provided there is no specific reason why they should be removed,—have a right to be present for the purpose of hearing what is going on." In 1913 the House of Lords frowned upon the holding of divorce proceedings *in camera*, stressing that it is important that the administration of justice take place in open court, though exceptions were recognized, as in cases involving wards, lunatics, or trade secrets.[21] Lord Atkinson observed, "The hearing of a case in public may be, and often is, no doubt, painful, humiliating, or deterrent both to parties and witnesses, and in many cases, especially those of a criminal nature, the details may be so indecent as to tend to injure public morals, but all this is tolerated and endured, because it is felt that in public trial is to be found, on the whole, the best security for

19. Magistrates' Courts Act, 1952, s. 98 (4). The sixth amendment of the U.S. Constitution guarantees a public trial, and it has been held that such a trial is a requirement of due process: *In re* Oliver, 333 U.S. 257 (1948).

20. Daubney v. Cooper (1829) 10 B. & C. 237, 109 E.R. 438 (K.B.).

21. Scott v. Scott, [1913] A.C. 417 (H.L.).

the pure, impartial, and efficient administration of justice, the best means for winning for it public confidence and respect." [22]

But even in this case the House of Lords noted that there are exceptions to the rule of public trial in matrimonial cases; for, as Lord Haldane pointed out, the general principle that courts must administer justice in public is subject to "a yet more fundamental principle that the chief object of Courts of justice must be to secure that justice is done." [23] And he noted that there are situations where the court is obliged to exclude the public in order that justice may be done. This issue has often arisen in regard to matrimonial cases, and it is now well established that the judge has discretion to bar the public, as, for example, when the wife finds it impossible to give her evidence because of the presence of people in the courtroom. [24]

Matrimonial cases, of course, are not criminal cases, but in the criminal law field there are comparable exceptions to the general rule in favor of public trials. For example, a judge of Assize has the authority to order the courtroom cleared if that expedient is necessary for the preservation of due quiet. [25] In 1917 the High Court gave its approval to the holding of a trial by a field general court-martial to which neither the public nor the press were admitted. [26] The accused had

22. *Id.* at 463.

23. *Id.* at 437.

24. Moosbrugger v. Moosbrugger (1913) 29 T.L.R. 658 (D.P. & A.). See also A. v. A. (1875) L.R. 3 P. & D. 230, 23 W.R. 386; D. v. D., [1903] P. 144; Cleland v. Cleland (1913) 109 L.T. 744 (D.P. & A.). For a similar holding in cases involving lunatics and wards see *Re* Martindale, [1894] 3 Ch. 193.

25. *Re* Sheriff of Surrey (1860) 2 F. & F., 234, 175 E.R. 1038 (N.P.).

26. *Ex parte* Doyle, [1917] 2 K.B. 254.

been arrested in Dublin in 1916 during the Irish Rebellion, and actual fighting was still going on. The Lord Chief Justice, Lord Reading, declared that every court has inherent jurisdiction to exclude the public where it is necessary in order to administer justice, and in view of the conditions of unrest and widespread disturbances still going on, there was danger of an attempt to terrorize the court.[27] Justice Darling also pointed out that it was "perfectly notorious" that witnesses who gave public testimony against rebels would have been made to suffer afterwards.[28]

There are a few statutes which specifically authorize courts to conduct proceedings *in camera*. The several Official Secrets Acts [29] authorize the court, on the request of the prosecution, to bar the public where publication of the evidence would be prejudicial to the national safety. A 1933 statute provides that when a child or young person is called as a witness in a proceeding relating to an offense against decency or morality, the court may exclude all persons from the courtroom except officers of the court, the parties and their lawyers, persons otherwise directly concerned in the case, and newsmen.[30] Except with leave of the

27. *Id.* at 271.

28. *Id.* at 274.

29. Official Secrets Act, 1911; Official Secrets Act, 1920, s. 8 (4); Official Secrets Act, 1939. Cf. *Ex parte* Norman (1915) 85 L.J.K.B. 203, 25 Cox C.C. 263, which upheld a proceeding held *in camera*, under Defence of the Realm Regulation 27, issued under the Defence of the Realm Act, 1914, in which the justice ordered the destruction of certain documents on the ground that they were forbidden. It was noted that this was not a criminal trial. On the main issue the court pointed out that since the object of the proceedings was to suppress the publication of certain documents in the interest of public safety, a hearing in public of this sort of matter would bring about the very mischief that the proceedings were intended to prevent.

30. Children and Young Persons Act, 1933, s. 37.

court, the general public is not permitted to attend proceedings in a juvenile court [31] or in a Domestic Proceedings Court.[32]

The exceptions to the general rule are neither numerous nor unusual, and the principle of the open public court is well established. In a wholly informal way the judge customarily suggests that women leave the court when evidence is given relating to sexually indecent events.[33] But for good cause, if the administration of justice so requires, the judge has discretionary authority to conduct a criminal trial, or part of it, *in camera.*

The Concept of Natural Justice

English judges can and do resort to the concept of natural justice, particularly where the absence of specific statutory directives allows them scope for the affirmation of general principles of justice. In a recent address, Professor Goodhart has explained:

What Parliament says is binding on all judges, and there is nothing more to be said about it. Judges, however, usually manage to get their own way: the House of Lords has been able to attain some of the same results which, in the United States, are achieved by the first Ten Amendments. By a convenient fiction it assumes that Parliament always intends that its statutes will accord with natural justice; no statute will therefore be construed to be retrospective or to deprive a person of a fair hearing or to prevent freedom of speech unless Parliament has so provided in the most specific terms.[34]

31. *Ibid.,* s. 47. Children under fourteen years of age may not be present in court as spectators: *ibid.,* s. 36.

32. Magistrates' Courts Act, 1952, s. 57.

33. See W. J. Williams, ed., *Moriarity's Police Law* (16th ed.; London: Butterworth, 1961), p. 39.

34. A. L. Goodhart, "Legal Procedure and Democracy," [1964] Camb. L.J. 52. See also E. B. Simmons, Q.C., "Natural Justice" (1963) 127 J.P. & L.G. Rev. 109–11.

Generally speaking, the concept of natural justice has been most frequently applied in civil or non-criminal cases. It is well established, for example, that the principle of natural justice requires administrative boards to give hearings to affected parties, although judicial procedures need not necessarily be employed.[35] A licensing board violated natural justice when it struck a doctor from the register after a hearing in which he was not permitted to present new evidence of his own, because no one should be condemned without being given a proper and fair chance to defend himself.[36] A union violates natural justice if it takes action against a member without giving him previous notice of the charge.[37] It is improper for a quasi-judicial tribunal to hear the advice of a medical specialist after the hearing, for the affected party must have a chance to comment on such evidence.[38] Similarly, a district council may not issue a clearance order determining the liabilities of a property owner without first giving him notice and a hearing.[39] In a widely noted case decided by the House of Lords in 1963, the summary removal from his position as a chief constable by the watch committee, without giving him an opportunity to be heard, was held to be

35. Cooper v. Wandsworth Board of Works (1863) 14 C.B.N.S. 180, 143 E.R. 414 (C.P.); Board of Education v. Rice (1911) 75 J.P. 393 (H.L.); Local Government Board v. Arlidge (1915) 79 J.P. 97 (H.L.); Errington v. Minister of Health (1935) 99 J.P. 15 (C.A.); R. v. Huntingdon Confirming Authority (1929) 93 J.P. 81 (C.A.).

36. General Council of Medical Education and Registration of the United Kingdom v. Spackman, [1943] 2 All E.R. 337 (H.L.).

37. Annamunthodo v. Oilfield Workers' Trade Union, [1961] 3 All E.R. 621 (P.C.).

38. R. v. Deputy Industrial Injuries Commissioner, [1962] 2 All E.R. 430 (Q.B.D.).

39. Hoggard v. Worsborough U.D.C., [1962] 1 All E.R. 468 (Sheffield Assizes).

unlawful as contrary to natural justice.[40] Lord Reid rejected the argument that natural justice is so vague as to be practically meaningless; he regarded this argument as "tainted by the perennial fallacy that because something cannot be cut and dried or nicely weighed or measured therefore it does not exist." [41] In fact, he thought that the concept of natural justice was more definite than the idea of negligence. Lord Hodson also rejected the claim that the natural justice concept was too vague. He said that no one would dispute the proposition "that three features of natural justice stand out—(1) the right to be heard by an unbiased tribunal; (2) the right to have notice of charges of misconduct; (3) the right to be heard in answer to those charges." [42]

The concept of natural justice has been applied to criminal law cases in a variety of situations. In a very recent case the Queen's Bench divisional court held that it was illegal for justices, sitting as a court of summary jurisdiction, to dismiss a charge of assault after a hearing, and then to bind the witnesses over, without first

40. Ridge v. Baldwin, [1964] A.C. 40, 2 W.L.R. 935 (H.L.). For comment on this case see A. L. Goodhart, "Ridge v. Baldwin: Administration and Natural Justice," 80 L.Q. Rev. 105–16 (January, 1964); A. W. Bradley, "A Failure of Justice and Defect of Police," [1964] Camb. L.J. 83–107; D. G. T. Williams, "The Dismissal of a Chief Constable," [1962] Crim. L. Rev. 613–21. For similar cases involving the improper dismissal of police officers, see Cooper v. Wilson, [1937] 2 All E.R. 726 (C.A.); Kanda v. Government of Malaya, [1962] 2 W.L.R. 1153 (P.C.).

41. [1964] A.C. 64–65.

42. [1964] A.C. 132. Lord Denning said, in Kanda v. Government of Malaya, [1962] 2 W.L.R. 1153, 1161 (P.C.). "If the right to be heard is to be a real right which is worth anything, it must carry with it a right in the accused man to know the case which is made against him. He must know what evidence has been given and what statements have been made affecting him; and then he must be given a fair opportunity to correct or contradict them."

informing them that this was in their minds and without giving them a chance to be heard on the matter.[43] Lord Parker, the Lord Chief Justice, declared that it is "elementary justice" that the judges should warn a witness what was in their minds and give him an opportunity to be heard. The justices acted "contrary to natural justice," Lord Parker said, since they failed to give the accused notice of charges and a chance to make answer. In another case, the justices retired, after conviction, to consider sentence, and at this point called in one of the adverse witnesses and interviewed him privately.[44] Though it may have been done from the best of motives, the appeal court held that this was a denial of natural justice. Said Lord Goddard, the Lord Chief Justice, "Time and time again this court has said that justice must not only be done but must manifestly be seen to be done. If justices interview a witness in the absence of the accused, justice is not seen to be done, because the accused does not and cannot know what was said." [45] An even stronger case was decided in 1962 when, after the prosecution's case had been heard, and after the defendant's solicitor had addressed the bench, the justices mistakenly thought that the solicitor had made a closing speech and so proceeded to find the case proved.[46] The appeal court ruled that the right to give evidence is fundamental, and that the accused had been denied natural justice since he had had no opportunity to be heard.

There have in recent years been several criminal cases where the question of natural justice arose in con-

43. Sheldon v. Bromfield Justices, [1964] 2 All E.R. 131 (Q.B.D.).
44. R. v. Bodmin Justices, [1947] K.B. 321, [1947] 1 All E.R. 109.
45. *Id.* [1947] K.B. 325.
46. R. v. Birkenhead Justices, *Ex parte* Fisher (1962) 106 S.J. 856 (Q.B.D.).

nection with the relations between the justices and their clerks. In 1962, the Queen's Bench divisional court ruled that it was improper for the clerk, at the conclusion of a hearing on a larceny charge, to hand up to the chairman a highly prejudicial note containing an argument for conviction, without showing it, as demanded, to the defendant's solicitor.[47] Lord Parker said it was most irregular that the clerk should try to influence the decision of the justices, and that the chairman should have refused to accept the note at that juncture. It is well established, he noted, that justices should never consult the clerk on the question of the guilt or innocence of the accused. The clerk may not retire with the justices, and passing a note to them immediately before they retired amounted to the same thing.

It has often been held that it is contrary to the concept of natural justice for the justices to permit the clerk to accompany them when they retire to consider their decision.[48] The decision must be that of the justices alone, Lord Goddard said in one of these cases, and "it is important to bear in mind that justice must not only be done but must be manifestly seen to be done. If it appears that there has been an opportunity for information to be given to the justices apart from that proved in open court, doubts may arise whether the trial has been fair."[49] Indeed, the Queen's Bench divisional court in 1953 issued a special practice note calling attention to the impropriety of the clerk's accompanying

47. R. v. Stafford Borough Justices (1962) 106 S.J. 199, [1962] 1 All E.R. 540 (Q.B.D.).

48. R. v. East Kerrier Justices, [1952] 2 Q.B. 719, [1952] 2 All E.R. 144 (Q.B.D.); R. v. Welshpool Justices, [1953] 2 All E.R. 807 (Q.B.D.); R. v. Barry (Glamorgan) Justices, [1953] 2 All E.R. 1005 (Q.B.D.).

49. R. v. Barry (Glamorgan) Justices, [1953] 2 All E.R. 1005 (Q.B.D.).

the justices when they retire to consider their decisions.[50] Lord Goddard pointed out that it is proper for the justices to consult their clerks on questions of law, on questions of mixed law and fact, on matters of practice and procedure, and on sentence practice. "In no circumstances, however," said Lord Goddard, "may justices consult their clerk as to the guilt or innocence of the accused, so far as it is simply a question of fact. . . ." They may consult with the clerk on the construction of a statute or regulation, or on whether the facts found constitute an offense; they may ask the clerk to refresh their memory as to any matter of evidence, and they may consult him about his notes. But they must not ask the clerk his opinion as to what sentence should be imposed, though they may ask him which penalties the law allows. In the last analysis, "the decision of the court must be the decision of the justices, and not that of the justices and their clerk. . . ."

In many ways the concept of natural justice is comparable to the American doctrine of due process of law. An English barrister recently wrote that the concept comes to this essentially:

(1) No man may seem to act as judge in his own cause.
(2) Every accused person has a right to hear the whole case against him.
(3) No man may be condemned unheard.[51]

This is not the whole of due process, of course, but it is a good part of it.

Right to Counsel

While at the common law a person accused of a misdemeanor always had the right to be represented by

50. [1953] 2 All E.R. 1306, per Lord Goddard, C.J.
51. Simmons, Q.C., "Natural Justice" (1963) 127 J.P. & L.G. Rev. 109, 110.

counsel, a rule long prevailed in England that in all other cases, where the accused most needed the assistance of a lawyer, he had no such right. The general theory was that the judge would see to it that the defendant was given a fair trial,[52] and no less a jurist than Lord Coke took the position that the Crown would not charge the commission of a crime unless the evidence was "so clear and manifest" that there could be no defense.[53] Long criticized, this harsh rule was ultimately corrected by Parliament. A statute was adopted in 1695 extending the right of representation by counsel to persons accused of treason,[54] and in 1836 the right was secured for all persons accused of felony.[55]

While the accused has a right to the assistance of counsel in his behalf, counsel may not be forced upon him against his will; but if he does have counsel, and counsel has examined witnesses and addressed the jury, then the prisoner is not free to supplement his advocate by addressing the court himself [56] or by revoking his lawyer's authority.[57] One may be put to trial without counsel, if he so chooses,[58] but the Court of Criminal Appeal has served warning that where a prisoner is not defended and an irregularity occurs at the trial, it is the judge's duty to inform the accused that he has a right

52. Joseph Chitty, *Criminal Law* (5th Am. ed. 1847), I, 406.

53. Sir Edward Coke, *The Third Part of the Institutes of the Laws of England* (London, 1797), Chap. 2, p. 29.

54. Treason Act, 1695, s. 1.

55. Trials of Felony Act, 1836, s. 1. The right to counsel is now deeply rooted in American constitutional law: Powell v. Alabama, 287 U.S. 45 (1932); Gideon v. Wainwright, 372 U.S. 335 (1963).

56. R. v. Woodward, [1944] K.B. 118, [1944] 1 All E.R. 159 (C.C.A.).

57. R. v. Maybury (1865) 11 L.T. 566 (Q.B.), Cockburn, C.J., said, "when a case is fairly before the court and counsel is seised of it, his authority cannot be revoked."

58. R. v. Elton (1942) 28 Cr. App. R. 126 (C.C.A.).

to submit that the trial should not continue.[59] Where, however, an accused person does have counsel, but owing to a misunderstanding the lawyer is not in court, and where counsel for the prosecution has suggested the appointment of some other member of the Bar then in the courtroom, it is error for the judge to proceed to the trial with the accused wholly unrepresented, since this is tantamount to depriving the defendant of the right to counsel, to which he is entitled by the law of the country.[60] Similarly, where a prisoner has secured counsel to conduct an appeal, and the advocate through no fault of his own was unable to reach the court in time to do so, to require the accused to present his own appeal is in substance to disregard the right of appeal.[61] Said Viscount Maugham: "The importance of persons accused of a serious crime having the advantage of counsel to assist them before the courts cannot be doubted by anybody who remembers the long struggle which took place in this country and which ultimately resulted in such persons having the right to be represented by counsel. . . ."[62]

The right to counsel clearly implies that the accused always has a right to confer with his lawyer.[63] Prior to the enactment of the Indictable Offences Act, 1848, section 17, however, it was held that justices had a discretion to admit or exclude advocates at the preliminary

59. R. v. Featherstone (1942) 28 Cr. App. R. 176 (C.C.A.).

60. R. v. Kingston (1948) 32 Cr. App. R. 183 (C.C.A.).

61. Galos Hired v. R., [1944] A.C. 149 (P.C.).

62. *Id.* at 155. While a private prosecutor has the right to engage counsel, Lord Parker, the Lord Chief Justice, recently ruled that justices need not order payment of counsel costs by defendants on their conviction where counsel was really unnecessary because of the trivial nature of the case, such as a case involving shoplifting. R. v. Feltham Justices, *Ex parte* Waitrose (1963) 107 S.J. 256 (Q.B.D.).

63. R. v. Machin, *The Times*, March 12, 1963 (C.C.A.).

examination.[64] Thus the Lord Chief Justice, Lord Tenterden, declared in 1831 that "the ends of justice will be sufficiently well attained in these summary proceedings by hearing only the parties themselves and their evidence, without that nicety of discussion, and sublety of argument, which are likely to be introduced by persons more accustomed to legal questions." [65] This view was abandoned in 1848. The controlling statute is now the Magistrates' Courts Act, 1952, section 99, which provides that "a party to any proceedings before a magistrates' court may be represented by counsel or solicitor. . . ." This right to have the assistance of counsel at the preliminary hearing implies that the lawyer has a right to cross-examine prosecution witnesses.[66]

One of the most attractive aspects of English criminal justice is the assurance of the assistance of counsel, at state expense, to indigent persons. Legal aid of this sort began with the enactment of the Poor Prisoner's Defence Act, 1903, which applied, however, only to trials on indictment.[67] The Poor Prisoner's Defence Act, 1930, extended this aid to include committal proceedings and summary trials, as well as trials on indictment. The present basic statute is the Legal Aid and Advice Act, 1949.[68] Other legislation provides for free legal repre-

64. R. v. Staffordshire Justices (1819) 1 Chit. 217 (K.B.); R. v. Borron (1820) 3 B. & A. 432, 106 E.R. 721 (K.B.); Cox v. Coleridge (1822) 1 B. & C. 37, 107 E.R. 15 (K.B.).

65. Collier v. Hicks (1831) 2 B. & Ad. 663, 109 E.R. 1290 (K.B.).

66. R. v. Griffiths and Williams (1886) 54 L.T. 280 (Beaumaris Assizes).

67. See Robert Egerton, *Legal Aid* (London: Paul, Trench, Trubner, 1945), pp. 20–22. See also Lord Parker, "The Development of Legal Aid in England since 1949," 40 Am. B.A.J. 1029–33 (1962).

68. The Court of Criminal Appeal has observed that legal aid should always be granted to a person liable to deportation. R. v. Sullivan, [1964] Crim. L. Rev. 120 (C.C.A.).

sentation for convicted persons in appeals to Quarter Sessions,[69] to the Court of Criminal Appeal (from Quarter Sessions, the Crown courts, the Central Criminal Court, or Courts of Assize),[70] and to the House of Lords.[71]

Legal aid is granted by the court before or at the trial on application of the accused or his solicitor and, if granted, is entirely free.[72] The defendant applies to the court for either a legal aid certificate, which gives him the services of a solicitor for summary cases or committal proceedings in indictable cases (or a solicitor and counsel in cases of preliminary hearings on murder charges), or a defense certificate, which gives a person who has been committed for trial for an indictable offense the services of both a solicitor and counsel.[73] Legal aid is available even if the prisoner pleads guilty.[74]

69. Summary Jurisdiction (Appeals) Act, 1933, as amended by Legal Aid and Advice Act, 1949, part II.

70. Criminal Appeal Act, 1907, s. 10, as amended by Legal Aid and Advice Act, 1949, part II. The Court of Criminal Appeal recently held that it is clear, under Regulation 6 of the Poor Prisoners' Defence (Defence Certificate) Regulations, 1960 (S.I. 1960, No. 260), that when a solicitor is assigned under a defense certificate, he can undertake any work necessary to give notice of appeal; the certificate does not lapse as soon as the conviction is recorded, and the solicitor does not have to wait for further instructions. R. v. Mullins, [1962] 3 All E.R. 237 (C.C.A.).

71. Administration of Justice Act, 1960, s. 8. The Court of Criminal Appeal may grant legal aid to a defendant on an appeal to the House of Lords, whether the defendant is the appellant or the respondent. See R. v. Daines and Williams (1960) 45 Cr. App. R. 57 (C.C.A.).

72. The elaborate system of legal aid in civil cases is wholly apart from that available in criminal cases.

73. See Poor Prisoners' Defence (Defence Certificate) Regulations, 1963 (No. 36); Poor Prisoners' Defence (Legal Aid Certificate) Regulations, 1963 (No. 37).

74. In a recent address to a meeting of magistrates, the Lord Chief Justice, Lord Parker, said, "It is sometimes said that in the case of prisoners who are going to plead guilty there must be but few cases

The certificate is granted, at the discretion of the judge or magistrate of the court where the case is to be heard, on two conditions. The judge must find that the certificate is desirable in the interests of justice, and that the defendant's means appear to be insufficient. If the case is in a magistrates' court, the charge must be serious or there must be exceptional circumstances. Aid must be granted, however, in cases involving the charge of murder if the defendant's means are insufficient. There is no fixed formula for determining "insufficiency," and the standard seems to vary from court to court. Actually, a strict means test is not applied, and the prevailing statute provides that if, on a question of granting a person free legal aid, "there is a doubt whether his means are sufficient to enable him to obtain legal aid or whether it is desirable in the interests of justice that he should have free legal aid, the doubt shall be resolved in favour of granting him free legal aid." [75]

Remuneration for work done in magistrates' courts is assessed by one of the twelve Legal Aid Area Commit-

where it is desirable in the interests of justice that he should have legal aid. With that I am afraid that I entirely disagree. I would myself put it the other way round and say that even in the case of pleas of guilty there will seldom be a case where it is not desirable in the interests of justice. Speaking for myself, I often get the feeling on the first day of Assizes when pleas are taken, that I am not getting all the help that I need in order to sentence the prisoner. I welcome a case in which there has been a full opportunity for solicitor and counsel to get to know and so be able to present the prisoner's background and character." Home Office Circular No. 90/1961, *Legal Aid in Criminal Cases*, Appendix A.

75. Legal Aid and Advice Act, 1949, s. 18 (1). For an argument that the accused is left at the mercy of the trial court, so far as securing legal aid is concerned, see Peter Benenson, *The Future of Legal Aid* (London: Fabian Research Series, No. 191, 1957), p. 29. Mr. Benenson is Chairman of the Legal Aid Subcommittee of the Society of Labour Lawyers.

tees of The Law Society. In all other cases, the fees of both solicitors and barristers are assessed by the court. In all instances, the scales of payment are determined by regulations laid down by the Home Secretary and are intended to provide fair and reasonable compensation for the work done.[76] For example, under the 1963 regulations [77] the minimum fee for counsel assigned to an appellant by the Court of Criminal Appeal was raised from £8 13s. to £11. The standard fee for a short conference in connection with an appeal either to Quarter Sessions [78] or the Court of Criminal Appeal is now £2 7s. The basic fee for a solicitor ranges from a minimum of £8 8s. to a maximum of £78 15s., and for a barrister from £8 13s. to £64 10s., though in fact the lowest fee paid to counsel is now ten guineas (£10 10s.). The rules also provide, however, that where the established fees would not provide fair remuneration

76. The Legal Aid and Advice Act, 1949, s. 21, directed the Home Secretary, in making regulations relating to the payment of fees to solicitors and counsel representing poor persons, to "have regard to the principle of allowing fair remuneration according to the work actually and reasonably done." The first adequate fees were provided for only in 1960. For the operation of the new rules, see *Legal Aid in Criminal Proceedings,* First Report of the Working Party, Home Office, Lord Chancellor's Office (London: H.M.S.O., 1962), and *Legal Aid in Criminal Proceedings,* Final Report of the Working Party, Home Office, Lord Chancellor's Office (London: H.M.S.O., 1963). It should be noted that solicitors and counsel are reimbursed for travel expenses actually and reasonably incurred, and for other out-of-pocket expenses.

77. Criminal Appeal (Fees and Expenses) Regulations, effective Sept. 2, 1963 (S.I. No. 1310). See [1963] Crim. L. Rev. 713.

78. The Appeal Aid Certificate Rules, effective Sept. 2, 1963 (S.I. No. 1309). Mr. Benenson (*supra,* note 75), on p. 29, makes the familiar point that the fees are "ludicrously inadequate," that most lawyers shy away from such business, and that the system works at all only "because such is the under-employment in the legal profession that there are always some lawyers prepared to be briefed on Defence Certificates. . . ."

because of the exceptional length, complexity, or difficulty of a case, the court may disregard the established
scale of fees and allow one that will "represent fair
remuneration according to the work actually and reasonably done." [79]

The Clerk of the Peace for each Quarter Sessions is
required to keep a list of solicitors and barristers who
are willing to accept criminal legal aid cases. The
panel for the Central Criminal Court of London (Old
Bailey) is administered by The Law Society. Most barristers are willing to be on the panels, although many
solicitors are not. The poor defendant has no right to
select his own solicitor and counsel; the choice is for the
court to make, though in some cases the accused is
consulted and his choice taken into account. Where a
defense certificate has been refused, the judge may still
request counsel to defend, if he thinks it desirable that
the accused should be represented.[80]

It is worth noting that under the English legal aid system the legal profession is not nationalized.[81] Lawyers
are not subject to the control of a minister. All that has
occurred is that the government provides the money to
pay counsel fees. In large measure the legal aid system
is controlled by the lawyers themselves.

There is one other method available to a defendant
for securing counsel. Any prisoner who comes to court
without counsel can select any barrister who is robed
and present in court, except counsel for the prosecution,
and, on the prisoner's producing £2 4s. 6d., the barrister to whom he points, without naming him, is obliged

79. The Appeal Aid Certificate Rules, 1960 (No. 258), Rule 6.
80. Such appointed counsel is given the same fee that is payable to
counsel under defence certificates.
81. See Denning, *The Road to Justice*, pp. 48–51.

to conduct the defense for the proffered fee. This is known as a "dock brief." The use of dock briefs is quite unusual today, except for pleas in mitigation.[82] The General Council of the Bar, with the approval of the Lord Chief Justice, recently issued a policy statement with reference to dock briefs: "Counsel who has accepted a dock brief and finds he has conflicting commitments, still incurs the obligation to represent the accused unless, on his application to the Court, the Court relieves him of his obligation. In such circumstances he may expect the Court to be helpful. This statement does not derogate from the right of Counsel to demur to being selected for a dock brief if he is of opinion that an existing commitment precludes him from undertaking the brief.[83]

Double Jeopardy

There is an ancient maxim in English law which forbids the trial or punishment of a person twice for the same offense: "Nemo debet bis vexari pro una et eadem causa." In accordance with this rule of justice, a defendant may offer to an indictment the special pleas in bar of autrefois acquit, former acquittal, or autrefois convict, former conviction. (A pardon also constitutes a special plea in bar to an indictment.) It is a fundamental rule that, where one has been acquitted in a criminal case, a new trial cannot be held on the same charge,[84] and the same rule applies where there has been a con-

82. The Bar Council is currently considering abolishing dock briefs.
83. [1964] Crim. L. Rev. 529, in connection with R. v. Howes, [1964] 2 All E.R. 172 (C.C.A.).
84. R. v. Read (1660) 1 Lev. 9, 83 E.R. 271 (K.B.). It is not material whether the first acquittal was in a trial on indictment or in a summary trial. Wemyss v. Hopkins, (1875) L.R. 10 Q.B. 378. See

viction and a second trial is attempted for precisely the same offense. While protection against double jeopardy is spelled out in several statutes dealing with specified offenses,[85] the Criminal Procedure Act, 1851, section 28, provides generally that "In any Plea of autrefois convict or autrefois acquit it shall be sufficient for any Defendant to state that he has been lawfully convicted or acquitted (as the Case may be) of the said Offence charged in the Indictment." Furthermore, the Interpretation Act, 1889, section 33, still in effect in this language, provides that "Where an act or omission constitutes an offence under two or more Acts, or both under an Act and at common law, whether any such Act was passed before or after the commencement of this Act, the offender shall, unless the contrary intention appears, be liable to be prosecuted and punished under either or any of those Acts or at common law, but shall not be liable to be punished twice for the same offence."

It is well established that conviction or acquittal in

Norval Morris and Colin Howard, *Studies in Criminal Law* (Oxford: Clarendon Press, 1964), Chap. 7.

There are a few exceptional situations when appeal may be had even where the accused won his case at the first level of justice. Thus, under the Administration of Justice Act, 1960, s. 13, a person convicted of contempt of court was given, for the first time, the right to appeal, but the act also gave the applicant for committal for contempt a right of appeal against a finding of not guilty. Generally speaking, there is no right of appeal against the dismissal of a complaint or information by a magistrate's court unless a statute expressly so provides. R. v. London County Keepers of the Peace and Justices (1890) 25 Q.B.D. 357. A few statutes do permit a right of appeal against dismissal, for example, the Customs and Excise Act, 1952, s. 283 (4), R. v. London Keepers of the Peace and Justices, [1945] K.B. 528, the Railway Rolling Stock Protection Act, 1872, s. 6, and the Diseases of Animals Act, 1950, s. 81.

85. Piracy Act, 1744, s. 2; Incitement to Mutiny Act, 1797, s. 2; Unlawful Oaths Act, 1797, s. 7, and 1812, s. 8; Treason Felony Act, 1848, s. 7.

a court of competent jurisdiction in a foreign country is a proper defense in an English court.[86] Similarly, if the action of an English court constitutes a defense, it must be shown that the court had jurisdiction over the case, for without jurisdiction the proceedings are plainly a nullity.[87] It has been held that a conviction is complete, and will therefore bar a later conviction for the same offense, even if it is not formally entered in the register,[88] and even though sentence has not been pronounced.[89] On the other hand, it is well established that acquittal on the ground of defective indictment will not bar a second trial.[90] Similarly, where the judge has discharged the jury, as, for failure to agree, there is no bar to a second trial;[91] and where a conviction has been reversed by an appellate court because of legal error, there is no bar to a subsequent indictment.[92] "The

86. R. v. Hutchinson (1677) 3 Keb. 785, 84 E.R. 1011 (K.B.); R. v. Roche (1775) 1 Leach 134, 168 E.R. 169 (C.C.); R. v. Aughet (1918) 13 Cr. App. R. 101 (C.C.A.); Sambasivam v. Public Prosecutor, Federation of Malaya (1950) 66 T.L.R. Pt. 2, 254 (P.C.).

87. R. v. Simpson [1914] 1 K.B. 66; R. v. Flower (1956) 40 Cr. App. R., 189, 193 (C.C.A.); R. v. West (1962) 46 Cr. App. R. 296 (C.C.A.). Cf. Haynes v. Davis, [1915] 1 K.B. 332.

88. R. v. Manchester Justices, [1937] 2 K.B. 96.

89. R. v. Sheridan (1936) 26 Cr. App. R. 1 (C.C.A.).

90. Anon. (1484) Jenk. 162, 145 E.R. 104 (Ex.); R. v. Vaux (1591) 2 Hale P.C. 251, 76 E.R. 992 (K.B.); Jones v. Givin (1713) Gilb. 185, 93 E.R. 300 (K.B.); R. v. Coogan (1787) 1 Leach 448, 168 E.R. 326 (C.C.), 2 East, P.C. 948; R. v. Reading (1793) 2 Leach 590, 168 E.R. 398 (C.C.); R. v. Bitton (1833) 6 Car. & P. 92, 172 E.R. 1159 (N.P.); R. v. Richmond (1843) 1 Car. & Kir. 240, 1 Cox C.C. 9, 174 E.R. 792 (N.P.).

91. R. v. Davison (1860) 2 F. & F. 250, 8 Cox C.C. 360 (C.C.C.); R. v. Charlesworth (1861) 1 B. & S. 460, 121 E.R. 786 (K.B.); R. v. Randall, [1960] Crim. C. & C. 154 (C.C.A.). The trial judge's discretion in discharging a jury is not subject to review by the Court of Criminal Appeal: R. v. Lewis (1909) 2 Cr. App. R. 180 (C.C.A.).

92. R. v. Drury (1849) 3 Car. & K. 193, 175 E.R. 517 (N.P.). Cf. R. v. Marsham *Ex parte* Pethick Lawrence, [1912] 2 K.B. 362. There

judgment reversed," said Coleridge, J., a century ago, "is the same as no judgment; upon a record without any judgment, no punishment can be suffered."[93] On the other hand, where there has been a verdict of acquittal, following a proper arraignment and the swearing in of a jury, there can be no second trial even though the verdict was obtained improperly.[94]

In England, when a person has been convicted of an offense, he may request the court, at the time of sentencing, to take into consideration other outstanding offenses on which he had not been charged or tried. The rule is that he is not entitled to plead autrefois convict in regard to these offenses, since there has been no conviction with respect to them.[95] It is the practice, however, and a desirable one, not to try the individual on outstanding offenses which had been taken into consideration by the court at his request.[96]

is a right to appeal from a trial court's rejection of the plea of autrefois convict even if a formal plea had not been made in the prescribed manner. R. v. Tonks, [1916] 1 K.B. 443 (C.C.A.).

93. R. v. Drury (1849) 3 Car. & K. 103, 100, 175 E.R. 516 (N.P.).

94. R. v. Middlesex Justices, *Ex parte* D.P.P., [1952] 2 All E.R. 312 (Q.B.D.). See also R. v. Duncan (1881) 7 Q.B.D. 198, 199, where Lord Coleridge, C. J., said, "The practice of the Courts has been settled for centuries, and is that in all cases of a criminal kind where a prisoner or defendant is in danger of imprisonment no new trial will be granted if the prisoner or defendant, having stood in that danger, has been acquitted." In this case it had been alleged that the first trial had been tainted by improper evidence and misdirection, and that the verdict was against the weight of evidence. The fact of acquittal was wholly controlling.

95. R. v. Nicholson (1947) 32 Cr. App. R. 98 (C.C.A.); R. v. Nicholson (No. 2) (1947) 32 Cr. App. R. 127 (C.C.A.). Here the Court of Criminal Appeal set aside a previous contrary holding by a Court of Assizes: R. v. McMinn (1945) 30 Cr. App. R. 138 (C.C.A.).

96. See John Frederick Archbold, *Pleading, Evidence and Practice in Criminal Cases*, T. R. F. Butler and Marston Garsia, eds. (34th ed.; London: Sweet & Maxwell, 1959), p. 156.

The main problem in respect to the special pleas of previous acquittal or conviction arises from the determination of the complicated issue of whether the two charges were substantially the same. "The test is not whether the facts relied upon are the same in the two trials, but whether there has been an acquittal of an offence which is the same, or practically the same, as that charged in the subsequent indictment."[97] Thus, a previous conviction for assault does not bar a later indictment for manslaughter, were the victim to die after the first conviction, since a new and different offense would arise if the victim died.[98] It has never been the law, Humphreys, J., once pointed out, that a person shall not be liable to be punished twice for the same act; the law is that he shall not be punished twice for the same offense.[99] Furthermore, where a person is accused of killing two people at the same time as a consequence of a single act, and he is tried for one murder and acquitted, there is no bar to a later trial for the other murder, since two separate offenses are involved.[100] Similarly, an acquittal on a charge of murder does not bar a later trial on a charge of administering poison with an intent to murder.[101]

There are many examples of situations where the

97. J. W. C. Turner, ed., *Kenny's Outline of Criminal Law* (17th ed.; Cambridge: Cambridge University Press, 1958), p. 564.

98. R. v. Morris (1867) 10 Cox C.C. 480 (C.C.A.); R. v. Friel (1890) 17 Cox C.C. 325 (Liverpool Assizes). The death is a new fact, and not merely a matter of aggravation.

99. R. v. Thomas, [1949] 2 All E.R. 662, [1950] 1 K.B. 26 (C.C.A.).

100. R. v. Dagnes (1839) 3 J.P. 293 (C.C.).

101. R. v. Connell (1853) 6 Cox C.C. 178 (C.C.C.). A conviction for willful neglect of a child is not a bar to a later trial for manslaughter. R. v. Tonks, [1916] 1 K.B. 443 (C.C.A.). An acquittal on a murder charge will not bar a later indictment for arson. R. v. Serné (1887) 16 Cox C.C. 311 (C.C.C.).

English courts have permitted second trials for different offenses arising from the same facts. An acquittal on a charge of rape will not bar a later indictment for assault with intent to commit rape [102] or for common assault.[103] An acquittal for murder will not bar a later trial for robbery,[104] and an acquittal for the offense of larceny will not bar an indictment for false pretense [105] or for illegal pawning.[106] Conviction for the crime of threatening to publish with intent to extort does not bar a prosecution, on the same evidence, for uttering a letter demanding money with menaces, since the offenses are not the same, or practically the same.[107] Acquittal for the possession of stolen goods will not bar a later prosecution for larceny of the same goods.[108] Acquittal on a charge of sodomy will not bar a later trial for committing an act of gross indecency, since the elements of the two offenses differ.[109] Similarly, acquittal of conspiracy to commit a crime does not justify the plea of autrefois acquit on the charge of aiding and abetting the commission of the crime, for the ingredients of the two offenses are different, notably in the element of previous agreement.[110] Finally, the High

102. R. v. Cisson (1847) 2 Car. & Kir. 781, 175 E.R. 327 (N.P.).
103. R. v. Dungey (1864) 4 F. & F. 99, 176 E.R. 485 (N.P.).
104. Connelly v. D.P.P. (1964) 108 S.J. 356, [1964] Crim. L. Rev. 477 (H.L.).
105. R. v. Henderson (1841) 1 Car. & Mar. 328, 2 Mood. C.C. 192, 5 J.P. 195, 174 E.R. 529 (N.P.).
106. Pickford v. Corsi, [1901] 2 K.B. 212, 19 Cox C.C. 712.
107. R. v. Kendrick and Smith (1931) 23 Cr. App. R. 1 (C.C.A.).
108. Flatman v. Light, [1946] K.B. 414.
109. R. v. Barron, [1914] 2 K.B. 570 (C.C.A.).
110. R. v. Kupferberg (1918) 13 Cr. App. R. 166 (C.C.A.). Cf. R. v. Baillie (1684) 10 St. Tr. 647 (P.C.), holding that a conviction for refusing to take an oath concerning the harboring of rebels will not stand in the way of a subsequent indictment for conspiracy to raise the same rebellion.

Court ruled in 1920 that the acquittal of the licensee of an inn on a charge of violating the Licensing Act, 1910, by allowing use of his premises contrary to the Betting Act, 1853, will not bar a later trial on the charge of violating the Betting Act by using his premises, whether licensed or not, as an occupier for the purpose of betting with persons resorting thereto.[111] The Court reasoned that the one offense can be committed only by the holder of a license for the retail sale of intoxicating liquor, while the other could be committed by one who did not hold such a license. Thus the two offenses were separate and distinct.

The case of *R. v. Connelly,* decided by the Court of Criminal Appeal in 1963 [112] and affirmed by the House of Lords in 1964,[113] pointed up several issues involved in the concept of former jeopardy. Connelly had been charged in separate indictments with murder and with robbery on the basis of the same incident. He was first put to trial on the murder charge, and his defenses were alibi and lack of intent to kill. Convicted of murder, he appealed successfully to the Court of Criminal Appeal on the ground of misdirection on the question of whether he had been present (the alibi defense). Nevertheless, the Court of Criminal Appeal gave leave for proceedings on the robbery indictment, and on the trial for robbery he unsuccessfully advanced a plea of autrefois acquit. The court dismissed his second appeal, pointing out that when it quashes a conviction, and enters a judgment of acquittal, it does not arrive at any specific finding regarding any of the ingredients of the

111. Bannister v. Clarke, [1920] 3 K.B. 598.

112. [1963] 3 W.L.R. 839, [1963] 3 All E.R. 510, [1964] Crim. L. Rev. 63 (C.C.A.).

113. Connelly v. D.P.P. (1964) 108 S.J. 356, [1964] Crim. L. Rev. 477 (H.L.).

offense. Its decision to quash merely means that the appellant is to be treated as if the jury had acquitted him, and thus it follows that he could not be charged a second time with the crime of murder. At the first trial the jury decided that Connelly had been present at the scene of the crime, but the Court of Criminal Appeal, in setting aside the judge's direction to the jury on the alibi issue, did not substitute a finding of fact of its own on this point. It merely held that the judge's charge had been unsatisfactory. Thus there is no inconsistency between the two decisions, since the acquittal on the murder charge did not involve a finding that Connelly was not proved to have been present at the crime.

The House of Lords agreed, holding that the test as to whether the appellant could rely upon the plea autrefois acquit was whether such proof as was necessary to convict for the second offense would establish guilt for the first offense. Nevertheless, the court also said that the practice of not joining a second charge with a count for murder is inconvenient and ought to be changed. The court took the position that, unless it would be unfair to the accused, the prosecutor should combine in a single indictment all the charges he intends to prefer.[114]

It remains to be noted that there have been many cases where a conviction or acquittal was held to bar another trial. Thus, a conviction for manslaughter will bar a later trial for murder.[115] A conviction on the charge of assault will bar a later prosecution for inflicting griev-

114. It was pointed out that this would be in accord with the Indictments Act, 1915, Sched. I, r. 3, which calls for a joinder of all charges that "are founded on the same facts or are a part of a series of offences of the same or a similar character."

115. R. v. Tancock (1876) 34 L.T. 455, 13 Cox C.C. 217 (Somerset Assizes). See also 2 Hale P.C. 246.

ous bodily harm,[116] for wounding with intent to murder,[117] for felonious wounding,[118] or for felonious stabbing.[119] Similarly, previous acquittal for murder committed in the perpetration of a burglary will bar later prosecution for burglary with violence, since the acquittal on the charge of murder is an answer to the allegation of violence.[120] Acquittal on a charge of joint felony bars a later indictment for a several felony.[121] Conviction on the charge of obtaining credit for goods by false pretenses bars later conviction for larceny of the same goods.[122]

116. R. v. Grimwood (1896) 60 J.P. 809, 13 T.L.R. 70 (Lewes Assizes).

117. R. v. Stanton (1851) 17 L.T.O.S. 280, 5 Cox C.C. 324 (Worcester Assizes).

118. R. v. Miles (1890) 24 Q.B.D. 423, 17 Cox C.C. 9 (C.C.R.). The court held there was jeopardy even though the defendant had been neither fined nor imprisoned, but was merely required to enter into recognizances to keep the peace. It is the conviction, and not the nature of the sentence, Lord Coleridge pointed out, which constitutes the bar to a later prosecution. Cf. R. v. Hogan, [1960] 3 All E.R. 149 (C.C.A.).

119. R. v. Walker (1843) 2 Mood. & Rob. 446, 174 E.R. 345 (N.P.): "it is clear, if he did not make the assault, he could not be guilty of that which includes and depends upon the assault."

120. R. v. Gould (1840) 9 C. & P. 364, 173 E.R. 870 (N.P.).

121. R. v. Dann (1835) 1 Mood. C.C. 424, 168 E.R. 1329 (C.C.R.).

122. R. v. King [1897] 1 Q.B. 214, 18 Cox C.C. 447 (C.C.R.). American constitutional law follows similar double jeopardy rules; see David Fellman, *The Defendant's Rights* (New York: Rinehart, 1958), Chap. 10.

V

Conduct of the Trial

The Jury

THE right of one accused of crime to be tried by a jury is deeply rooted in English law and practice.[1] Blackstone said that "trial by jury ever has been, and I trust ever will be, looked upon as the glory of the English law. . . . The liberties of England cannot but subsist so long as this palladium remains sacred and inviolate, not only from all open attacks (which none will be so hardy as to make), but also from all secret machinations, which may sap and undermine it by introducing new and arbitrary methods of trial. . . ."[2] Writing at about the same time, Lord Camden declared that "trial by jury is indeed the foundation of our free constitution; take that away, and the whole fabric will soon moulder into dust. These are the sentiments of my youth—inculcated by precept, improved by experience, and warranted by example."[3]

1. The grand jury was abolished by the Administration of Justice Act, 1933, s. 1 (1).
2. 3 Com. 379, 4 Com. 350.
3. Lord John C. Campbell, *Lives of the Lord Chancellors* (5th ed.), VII, 35.

While the jury system seems to be anchored securely in English law, some contemporary students are somewhat less enthusiastic in their evaluations of it. Glanville Williams recently reviewed the considerations on both sides of the debate over the jury system [4] and concluded that "notwithstanding the panegyrics on the jury, it occupies a comparatively minor place in the administration of criminal justice at the present day." [5] He noted that jury trial was too costly and cumbrous for minor offenses, and that in actual fact 84 per cent of all indictable offenses are tried summarily by the magistrates and only 16 per cent by juries. [6] Many indictable crimes can be tried summarily if the accused gives his consent. Most juveniles are tried by magistrates sitting in juvenile courts. Furthermore, the representativeness of the jury has been challenged as a result of the property qualification [7] and exemptions. "The jury," Sir Patrick Devlin has pointed out, "is not really representative of the nation as a whole. It is predominantly male, middle-aged, middle-minded and middle-class." [8]

While the English jury still includes the traditional number of twelve members, statute [9] provides that the trial may proceed, if a juror dies or is for some other reason incapable of serving or is discharged, provided that the number of jurors does not fall below ten. The Court of Criminal Appeal recently indicated that the proper practice is for both parties to give their consent

4. *The Proof of Guilt* (2nd ed.; London: Stevens, 1958), Chap. 10.
5. *The Proof of Guilt*, p. 264.
6. *The Proof of Guilt*, p. 266.
7. A juror must be the owner, in fee or for life, of lands or tenements worth £10 a year, or he must hold a long leasehold worth £20 a year, or occupy a house rated at £20 a year (£30 in Middlesex).
8. *Trial By Jury* (London: Stevens, 1956), p. 20.
9. Criminal Justice Act, 1925, s. 15.

in writing, in open court, to the continuance of the trial with fewer than twelve members.[10] The American practice of using alternate jurors is not followed, and the Criminal Law Revision Committee has rejected the suggestion that it be adopted.[11]

The right to an impartial jury includes the privilege of challenge.[12] By statute, the accused is entitled to seven peremptory challenges while the Crown has none.[13] Either side may challenge for cause on the ground that the prospective juror is not qualified to discharge the duties of a juror or is incapable of doing so because of personal defects. Many early cases upheld the right of the parties to challenge a prospective juror for not being impartial.[14] Counsel could not, however, examine a juror with a view to challenge without first stating some ground for the proceeding; lack of impartiality had to be proved by extrinsic evidence.[15]

10. R. v. Browne (1962), 46 Cr. App. R. 314 (C.C.A.).

11. Criminal Law Revision Committee, Fifth Report, *Criminal Procedure (Jurors)*, April, 1964, Cmd. 2349. The committee also recommended that it should be permitted to go forward with a trial with as few as nine jurors, and that the consent of the parties should be unnecessary except in trials for murder or for any offense punishable by death.

12. See John Frederick Archbold, *Pleading, Evidence and Practice in Criminal Cases*, T. R. F. Butler and Marston Garsia, eds. (34th ed.; London: Street & Maxwell, 1959), pp. 177–84.

13. Criminal Justice Act, 1948, s. 35 (1). Special juries were abolished in all criminal cases by the Juries Act, 1949, s. 18 (1).

14. R. v. Cook (1696) 13 St. Tr. 311, 333; R. v. D'Coigly (1798) 26 St. Tr. 1191, 1227; R. v. Swain (1838) 2 Mood. & Rob. 112, 174 E.R. 232 (N.P.); R. v. Geach (1840) 9 C. & P. 499, 173 E.R. 929 (N.P.); R. v. Martin (1848) 6 St. Tr. n.s. 925. One who served on a grand jury could be challenged for sitting on the trial jury for lack of impartiality. Titus Oates' Case (1685) 10 St. Tr. 1079, 1081.

15. R. v. Edmonds (1821) 4 B. & Ald. 471, 106 E.R. 1007 (K.B.); R. v. Stewart (1845) 1 Cox C.C. 174 (Kent Assizes); R. v. Dowling (1848) 3 Cox C.C. 509 (C.C.C.).

Actually, challenge for cause has become obsolescent; counsel generally takes up the matter in advance, informally, with the clerk of the court.[16]

The issue of jury impartiality may arise, however, on an appeal. The inability of a juror to understand English, for example, may well result in a miscarriage of justice that would justify setting aside the judgment of conviction.[17] On the other hand, the Court of Criminal Appeal recently held that a juror's knowledge of the defendant's character or previous convictions does not amount to an automatic disqualification; there has been no miscarriage of justice in the absence of evidence that the juror was prevented by his knowledge from listening to the evidence and giving the accused a fair trial.[18]

The independence of the jury was established in 1670 in *Bushell's Case*.[19] In an appeal heard in 1960, the Court of Criminal Appeal had occasion to underscore the importance of the jury's complete freedom to deliberate uninfluenced by any promise and unintimidated by any threat.[20] The charge was larceny and, after the jury had been out for over two hours, the judge called them back, saying he had another appointment and would leave the building in ten minutes. If the jurors did not reach a decision by then, he said, they would be kept all night. He also said that the case was a simple one which did not require much time for delib-

16. Sir Patrick Devlin, *Trial by Jury*, p. 29.
17. Ras Behari Lal v. R. (1933) 50 T.L.R. 1 (P.C.).
18. R. v. Box, [1964] 1 Q.B. 430 (C.C.A.).
19. Bushell's Case (1670) 6 St. Tr. 999, Vaughan 135, 124 E.R. 1006 (C.P.).
20. R. v. McKenna, [1960] 1 Q.B. 411, [1960] 1 All E.R. 326, [1960] 2 W.L.R. 306, [1960] Crim. L. Rev. 210 (C.C.A.). Cf. Jenkins v. United States, 380 U.S. 445 (1965).

eration, telling them to go back, use their common sense, and not worry about legal quibbles. The Court of Criminal Appeal quashed the conviction. The court ruled that, while it was understandable that the judge should experience irritation, it was insupportable for him to express it to the jury in the form of a threat. Said Cassels, J., "It is a cardinal principle of our criminal law that in considering their verdict, concerning, as it does, the liberty of the subject, a jury shall deliberate in complete freedom. . . . They still stand between the Crown and the subject, and they are still one of the main defences of personal liberty. To say to such a tribunal in the course of its deliberations that it must reach a conclusion within ten minutes or else undergo hours of personal inconvenience and discomfort, is a disservice to the cause of justice." [21]

Since the jury is independent, it follows that a court has no right, for reasons of public policy, to inquire into what occurred in the jury room.[22] Similarly, it is wholly improper for the judge or any other officer of the court to communicate with the jury privately or in any other way except in the presence of the parties and counsel in open court.[23] This is a very old rule. Thus, in a late seventeenth century case Peter Cook complained: [24]

21. [1960] 1 Q.B. 422. "The notoriety of the case is itself some indication that flagrant intimidation of juries is extremely rare in this country." 23 Mod. Law Rev. 306, 307 (1960).

22. R. v. Frank William George Thompson (1961) 46 Cr. App. R. 72, [1962] 1 All E.R. 65 (C.C.A.). The same rule applies to civil cases: Ellis v. Deheer, [1922] 2 K.B. 113. See "Sanctity of the Jury-Room," 107 Sol. J. 347–48 (1963).

23. R. v. Willmont, (1914) 10 Cr. App. R. 173 (C.C.A.); R. v. Green (1949) 34 Cr. App. R. 33 (C.C.A.); R. v. Furlong (1950) 34 Cr. App. R. 79 (C.C.A.); R. v. Davis (1960) 44 Cr. App. R. 235 (C.C.A.).

24. R. v. Cook (1696) 13 St. Tr. 311, 354.

Cook. My lord chief justice.

L.C.J. Treby. What say you, Mr. Cook?

Cook. My lord, if your lordship pleases, I desire the jury may not be talked to by any body; and I understand there are some talking with the jury.

L.C.J. Treby. Fy upon it! We will lay any body by the heels that do so; they must neither be disturbed, nor instructed by any body.

Cook. My lord, I am informed there was somebody talking to them, and telling them this was the same case with sir John Freind.

L.C.J. Treby. Do you but shew us the man, and we will find another place for him; we will send him to the gaol, I will assure you.

It is an ancient rule of English law, based on the principle that the jury's verdict must be free from reasonable doubt, that the jury's decision must be by unanimous vote.[25] It is now customary to drop a prosecution after two juries have disagreed.[26] In his instructions the judge may tell the jury that the verdict represents a collective judgment, that there must be argument and "a certain amount of give and take and adjustment of views. . . ."[27] Lord Goddard, the Lord Chief Justice, said that "jurors often have to be reminded that the case may be one in which some of them may start by taking one view and then, finding that the others are against them, may talk the matter over, subordinate their views to those of the majority and concur in the verdict. That is the only way in which juries can arrive at verdicts."[28] It is also permissible for the judge to remind the jury of the great public inconvenience and expense of not

25. See Sir Patrick Devlin, *Trial by Jury*, pp. 48–57.

26. *Trial by Jury*, p. 52.

27. R. v. Walhein (1952) 36 Cr. App. R. 167 (C.C.A.). See also R. v. Quartermaine (1919) 14 Cr. App. R. 109 (C.C.A.).

28. R. v. Walhein (1952) 36 Cr. App. R. 167, 168 (C.C.A.).

arriving at a verdict.[29] But while the judge may use fairly strong language in exhorting a jury to reach a verdict, he must be careful not to use phrases "which import a measure of coercion."[30] The judge must be careful, for example, not to give the jury the impression that it ought to convict.[31] Furthermore, a judge must not tell the jury that if a small minority of the jurors disagree with the others it is consistent with their oaths to decide they might be wrong and to accept the views of the majority.[32] Lord Hewart said that it is wrong to suggest to some members of the jury that they should accept views which they do not in fact accept merely for the sake of conformity and convenience. "It is fundamental," he asserted, "that a jury should agree, and by 'agree' is meant honestly agree, not make a colourable appearance of agreeing." Similarly, it is a misdirection for the judge to tell a jury, on the matter of unanimity, that, as in the case of committees, not all jurors always have to agree, for they might reach agreement in any case.[33] The Court of Criminal Appeal thinks that such a directive might give jurors the impression that the necessity for unanimity has in some measure been relaxed, and is no longer as important as it has been in the past.

The Burden of Proof

It is an elementary proposition of English law that a higher minimum of proof is necessary to support a

29. R. v. Walhein (1952) 36 Cr. App. R. 167 (C.C.A.).
30. Shonkatallie v. R., [1962] A.C. 81, 91 (P.C.) (Lord Denning).
31. R. v. Smithson (1963) 107 S.J. 813 (C.C.A.).
32. R. v. Mills (1939) 27 Cr. App. R. 80 [1939] 2 K.B. 90 (C.C.A.).
33. R. v. Davey (1960) 45 Cr. App. R. 11, [1960] 1 W.L.R. 1287 (C.C.A.).

criminal accusation than to support a civil charge. In civil cases it suffices that there is a "preponderance" of evidence in favor of the winning party.[34] In criminal cases the prosecution must prove the defendant guilty "beyond reasonable doubt." [35] One basis for this rule is the strength of the presumption of innocence, for English law always starts with a strong presumption against the commission of a crime.[36] An ancient maxim in the Roman law also supports this position on the burden of proof: *Ei incumbit probatio qui dicit, non qui negat,* which means that the burden of proof is on the party making the allegation and not on the party who denied it.[37] Furthermore, as a leading treatise makes the point, "history shows how necessary is some such rule, emphatic and universal, in order to protect prisoners from the credulity which the shifting currents of prejudice will inspire about any offence, or class of offences, that

34. The classic statement on the burden of proof in civil cases is that of Willes, J., in Cooper v. Slade, (1858) 6 H.L. Cas. 746, 772, 10 E.R. 1488, where the judge referred to the "elementary proposition that in civil cases the preponderance of probability may constitute sufficient ground for a verdict."

35. Lord Reading, the Lord Chief Justice, once said that the burden of proving the defendant guilty beyond a reasonable doubt "always rests upon the prosecution and never changes." R. v. Schama (1914) 79 J.P. 184, 24 Cox C.C. 591, 11 Cr. App. R. 45 (C.C.A.). See also R. v. Willshire (1881) 6 Q.B.D. 366. See C. B. Orr, "The Burden of Proof in Criminal Cases," (1952) 116 J.P. Jo. 499. Cf. comments of Justice Frankfurter in Leland v. Oregon, 343 U.S. 790, 802 (1952) (dissenting opinion).

36. See R. v. Twyning (1819) 2 B. & Ald. 386, 106 E.R. 407 (K.B.); Doe dem. Fleming v. Fleming (1827) 4 Bing. 266, 130 E.R. 769 (Com. Pl.); Morris v. Miller (1766) 1 W. Bl. 632 (K.B.); R. v. Cresswell (1876) 1 Q.B.D. 446. On the presumption of innocence see C. K. Allen, *Legal Duties* (Oxford: Clarendon Press, 1931), pp. 253–94.

37. H. A. Palmer and Henry Palmer, eds. *Wilshere's Criminal Procedure* (4th ed.; London: Street & Maxwell, 1961), p. 103.

may for the moment have aroused popular indignation." [38]

Accordingly, it is said in England that the more heinous the crime, the higher the minimum of necessary proof.[39] And since the prosecution has the obligation of proving its case, it follows that there ought not to be a conviction when the evidence is equally consistent with innocence and guilt.[40] Furthermore, it is a fatal error for the trial judge to fail to give the jury any direction at all on the onus of proof and on the fact that the accused is entitled to the benefit of a reasonable doubt.[41] Lord Atkin once pointed out that "unless the judge makes sure that the jury appreciate their duty in this respect his omission is as grave an error as active misdirection on the elements of the offence, and a verdict of guilty given by a jury who have not taken this fundamental principle into account is given in a case where the essential forms of justice have been disregarded." [42] He also made it clear that it did not suffice that counsel for the defense had instructed the jury on this point. "Jurors are apt to be suspicious of law propounded by the defence; they look to the judge for authoritative statement of it. . . ." [43]

38. J. W. C. Turner, ed., *Kenny's Outlines of Criminal Law* (17th ed.; Cambridge: Cambridge University Press, 1958), p. 479.

39. R. v. Hobson (1823) 1 Lew. C.C. 261, 168 E.R. 1033 (C.C.).

40. R. v. Bookbinder (1931) 23 Cr. App. R. 59 (C.C.A.); R. v. Turkington (1930) 22 Cr. App. R. 91 (C.C.A.).

41. R. v. Badash (1917) 13 Cr. App. R. 17, 26 Cox C.C. 155 (C.C.A.); Lawrence v. R., [1933] A.C. 699 (P.C.). See also R. v. Milne, [1961] Crim. L. Rev. 323 (C.C.A.); R. v. Murtagh and Kennedy (1955) 39 Cr. App. R. 72 (C.C.A.); R. v. Rees (1937) 21 Cr. App. R. 35 (C.C.A.); R. v. Deans, [1961] Crim. L. Rev. 631 (C.C.A.); R. v. Oliva (1960) 46 Cr. App. R. 241, [1961] Crim. L. Rev. 111 (C.C.A.).

42. Lawrence v. R., [1933] A.C. 699, 707, (P.C.).

43. *Ibid.*

It is also prejudicial error for the trial judge to tell the jury that because the evidence of the prosecution established a prima facie case, the burden of proof then shifted to the defendant.[44] The burden of proof in criminal cases always rests with the prosecution. In a recent case involving a stolen automobile, three pickax handles bound with adhesive tape were found in the car,[45] and the question arose whether or not the accused was also guilty of possessing offensive weapons. The accused testified that he didn't know that the handles were in the car, but the trial judge told the jury that the onus shifts to the defendant, once possession is proved, to show that he was in lawful possession. The Court of Criminal Appeal ruled that the instruction on the burden of proof was clearly wrong, since the onus was always on the Crown to prove that the accused knew that the pickax handles were in the car. Similarly, it has been established that it is wrong for the prosecutor to tell the jury that an acquittal of the defendant would virtually convict a complaining witness of perjury.[46] The court explained that all that an acquittal means is that the jury was not satisfied beyond a reasonable doubt that the accused committed the crime; it said that the jury should decide the case solely upon the weight and credibility of the evidence, and not with reference to the supposed consequences to one side or the other. The court added that counsel for the prosecution should regard themselves as ministers of justice, and should not be betrayed by feelings of professional rivalry or regard the trial as "a contest for skill and preeminence."

44. R. v. Stoddart (1909) 2 Cr. App. R. 217 (C.C.A.).
45. R. v. Cugullere (1961) 45 Cr. App. R. 108 (C.C.A.).
46. R. v. Puddick (1865) 4 F. & F. 497 (N.P.).

A decision in line with these principles came down from the House of Lords in 1935.[47] In this case the trial judge had instructed the jury that, since the accused had shot his wife, the law presumed him to be guilty of murder unless he could satisfy the jury that the death was due to an accident. The House of Lords ruled that this instruction was clearly wrong. "No matter what the charge or where the trial," Lord Sankey said, "the principle that the prosecution must prove the guilt of the prisoner is part of the common law of England and no attempt to whittle it down can be entertained." [48]

English appellate judges have ruled repeatedly that while it is the trial judge's duty to deal properly with the question of the burden of proof, it cannot be said "that any particular form of words is sacrosanct or absolutely necessary." [49] Furthermore, the Court of Criminal Appeal has on occasion declined to quash a conviction—even where the judge's direction had been defective—on the ground that there had been no substantial miscarriage of justice, in accordance with section 4 (1) of the Criminal Appeal Act, 1907, when other words or expressions had been used by the judge to suggest the point.[50]

The House of Lords has approved, in the past, of the judge's directing the jury in terms of proof beyond

47. Woolmington v. D.P.P., [1935] A.C. 462, 25 Cr. App. R. 72 (H.L.).

48. *Id.* [1935] A.C. at 481–82.

49. R. v. Blackburn (1955) 39 Cr. App. R. 84, 85 (C.C.A.). See also R. v. Rice, [1960] Crim. L. Rev. 630 (C.C.A.); R. v. Hepworth and Fearnley, [1955] 2 Q.B. 600 (C.C.A.).

50. R. v. Sparrow (1962) 46 Cr. App. R. 288 (C.C.A.); R. v. Slinger, [1961] Crim. L. Rev. 324 (C.C.A.); R. v. Woods, [1961] Crim. L. Rev. 324 (C.C.A.); R. v. Jones, [1961] Crim. L. Rev. 322 (C.C.A.); R. v. Attfield (1961) 45 Cr. App. R. 309 (C.C.A.); R. v. Jones, [1961] Crim. L. Rev. 322 (C.C.A.).

reasonable doubt.[51] But in 1952 the Court of Criminal Appeal rather abruptly turned against this test on the ground that "reasonable doubt" cannot be satisfactorily defined.[52] The Lord Chief Justice, Lord Goddard, said that it would be far better to tell the jury they must be "satisfied" so that they can "feel sure" of the defendant's guilt. But in 1955 the court went back to the older and more familiar test.[53] While it is still true that no particular set of words or phrases is indispensably necessary, trial judges must be careful to locate the onus of proof clearly and to get across to the jury the idea of reasonable doubt. Thus the Court of Criminal Appeal has disapproved of the trial judge's directing the jury to be "reasonably sure" of the defendant's guilt.[54] Ashworth, J., has declared, "It is not right to tell a jury that they must be reasonably sure. . . . It imports a standard of certainty below that which is conveyed by the now established direction that they must be satisfied so that they feel sure." [55] Accordingly, the court has

51. Woolmington v. D.P.P., [1935] A.C. 462, 481 (H.L.); R. v. Mancini, [1942] A.C. 1, 11–13 (H.L.). See Williams, *The Proof of Guilt*, Chap. 7.

52. R. v. Summers (1952) 36 Cr. App. R. 14 (C.C.A.).

53. R. v. Hepworth and Fearnley, [1955] 2 Q.B. 600 (C.C.A.); R. v. Murtagh and Kennedy (1955) 39 Cr. App. R. 72 (C.C.A.). See Glanville Williams, "The Direction of the Jury on the Burden of Proof," [1955] Crim. L. Rev. 464.

54. R. v. Head and Warrener (1961) 45 Cr. App. R. 225 (C.C.A.); R. v. Jones, [1961] Crim. L. Rev. 322 (C.C.A.).

55. R. v. Head and Warrener (1961) 45 Cr. App. R. 228 (C.C.A.). In R. v. Thomas (1960) 33 Austl. L.J. 413, the High Court of Australia held it a serious misdirection for the judge to tell the jury they should "come to a feeling of comfortable satisfaction that the accused is guilty." The court felt that it was dangerous to venture upon such a novel elucidation of the principle of criminal law relating to reasonable doubt, and that in this instance the jury might believe that the court had lessened the severity of the proper standard. See R. W. Cannon, "Beyond Reasonable Doubt," [1961] Crim. L. Rev. 235–41.

ruled that the phrase "reasonably satisfied" is adequate.[56] The court has also ruled that it is improper merely to direct the jury that they must be "satisfied" as to the guilt of the accused, without saying anything about the degree of satisfaction.[57] Similarly, it does not suffice to tell the jury they must be "pretty certain" of the defendant's guilt, since this gives the burden of proof a new direction.[58]

The principle that the burden of proof rests on the prosecution has many ramifications. It applies to cases where the accused offers such defenses as self-defense,[59] provocation,[60] or drunkenness.[61] It is not proper, in a murder case, for the judge to tell the jury that, where the accused advanced the defense of self-defense, the jury must be satisfied that the defense was necessary, because "the onus remains throughout upon the prosecution to establish that the accused is guilty of the crime. . . ."[62] Similarly, it is an error to direct the jury that the onus of proving an alibi is on the accused, and the Court of Criminal Appeal recently said that such a misdirection in law was "absolutely fundamental."[63] While the onus of proving duress, as a defense, is on the accused, the Court of Criminal Appeal has pointed out that all this means is that the accused has the onus

56. R. v. Kritz, [1950] 1 K.B. 82, 89 (C.C.A.).

57. R. v. Hadjimitsis, [1961] Crim. L. Rev. 563 (C.C.A.); R. v. Cave (1963) 107 S.J. 177 (C.C.A.).

58. R. v. Law, [1961] Crim. L. Rev. 52 (C.C.A.).

59. Chan Kau v. R., [1955] A.C. 206 (P.C.); R. v. Labell, [1957] 1 Q.B. 547 (C.C.A.).

60. R. v. Mancini, [1942] A.C. 1 (H.L.).

61. Beard v. D.P.P., [1920] A.C. 479 (H.L.).

62. Chan Kau v. R., [1955] A.C. 206, 211 (P.C.).

63. R. v. Johnson (1961) 46 Cr. App. R. 55, 58 (C.C.A.); R. v. Stebbing, [1962] Crim. L. Rev. 472 (C.C.A.); R. v. Denney, [1963] Crim. L. Rev. 191 (C.C.A.).

of introducing sufficient evidence on the point to warrant its submission to the jury; once the defendant has made duress a live issue, "it is then for the Crown to destroy that defence in such a manner as to leave in the jury's minds no reasonable doubt that the accused cannot be absolved on the grounds of the alleged compulsion." [64] While an "evidential" burden is cast on the defendant, the ultimate or "persuasive" burden of proof still rests with the prosecution. Similarly, while the burden of proof is on the defendant to prove insanity,[65] it is satisfied by evidence that will convince the jury of the probability of that which the accused is called upon to establish, and this burden is not as heavy as the burden of proof resting upon the prosecution.[66]

Some statutes put the onus specifically on the defendant to prove some fact, for example that he had a lawful excuse for carrying housebreaking implements at night.[67] But it has been held that where, either by statute or by common law, some matter is presumed against the defendant "unless the contrary is proved," the jury should be directed that the burden of proof on the accused is less than that required of the prosecution for proving the case beyond a reasonable doubt.[68]

64. R. v. Gill, [1963] 1 W.L.R. 841, 846 (C.C.A.).
65. Woolmington v. D.P.P., [1935] A.C. 462, 475 (H.L.).
66. Sodeman v. R., [1936] W.N. 190, [1936] 2 All E.R. 1138 (P.C.); R. v. Bentley, [1960] Crim. L. Rev. 777 (C.C.A.).
67. Larceny Act, 1916, s. 28 (2). See R. v. Ward, [1915] 3 K.B. 696. For other statutes, see Merchandise Marks Act, 1887, ss. 2, 6; Explosive Substances Act, 1883, s. 4; Forgery Act, 1913, ss. 8, 9, 10; Coinage Offences Act, 1936; Obscene Publications Act, 1857, s. 1, and see Cox v. Stinton, [1951] 2 K.B. 1021; Thomson v. Chain Libraries Ltd., [1954] 2 All E.R. 616 (Q.B.D.); Prevention of Corruption Act, 1916, s. 2, and see R. v. Carr-Briant, [1943] K.B. 607.
68. R. v. Carr-Briant, [1943] K.B. 607 (C.C.A.); Sodeman v. R., [1936] W.N. 190, [1936] 2 All E.R. 1138 (P.C.).

Comment by the Judge

The English judge is, generally speaking, an active participant in the trial. He has wide latitude in putting questions to witnesses, though the Court of Criminal Appeal has taken the position that it is undesirable for the judge to cross-examine a defendant, or any witness, during the examination-in-chief.[69] The court also takes the position that, where a judge does intervene, he should remind the jury that the question of believing or not believing any particular witness is for the jury to decide.[70] Furthermore, the judge has a duty to protect the rights of the accused even on his own initiative. Thus the House of Lords has ruled that it is the duty of the judge to bar inadmissible evidence offered by the prosecution even if counsel for the accused did not object.[71]

The English judge has the important and expansive function of summing up the case, after all the evidence is in, for the guidance of the jury. Lord Reading, the Lord Chief Justice, explained in a 1917 case that it was well established "that a judge, when directing a jury, is clearly entitled to express his opinion on the facts of the case, provided that he leaves the issues of fact to the jury to determine. A judge obviously is not justified in directing a jury, or using in the course of his summing up such language as leads them to think that he is directing them, that they must find the facts in the way which he indicates. But he may express a view that the

69. R. v. Bateman (1946) 31 Cr. App. R. 106 (C.C.A.).

70. R. v. Gilson (1944) 29 Cr. App. R. 174 (C.C.A.). See also R. v. Cain (1936) 25 Cr. App. R. 204 (C.C.A.). The judge should not interrupt the examination of witnesses so constantly as to make counsel's task impossible. R. v. Clewer (1953) 37 Cr. App. R. 37 (C.C.A.).

71. R. v. Stirland, [1944] A.C. 315, 327 (H.L.). See (1942) 58 L.Q. Rev. 383.

facts ought to be dealt with in a particular way, or ought not to be accepted by the jury at all. He is entitled to tell the jury that the prisoner's story is a remarkable one, or that it differs from accounts which he has given of the same matter on other occasions." [72] Similarly, the Court of Criminal Appeal once said, "In our view a judge is not only entitled, but ought, to give the jury some assistance on questions of fact as well as on questions of law. Of course, questions of fact are for the jury and not for the judge, yet the judge has experience on the bearing of evidence, and in dealing with the relevancy of questions of fact, and it is therefore right that the jury should have the assistance of the judge. It is not wrong for the judge to give confident opinions upon questions of fact. It is impossible for him to deal with doubtful points of fact unless he can state some of the facts confidently to the jury." [73] The court added that "when one is considering the effect of a summing-up, one must give credit to the jury for intelligence, and for the knowledge that they are not bound by the expressions of the judge upon questions of fact."

Nevertheless, the judge must be careful to include in his summing-up the defense of the accused, no matter how flimsy or unrealistic the defendant's story may be.[74] Furthermore, it is not permissible for the judge to say to the jury that the defense of the accused was absurd and that the accused was in fact guilty.[75] It is for the

---

72. R. v. O'Donnell (1917) 12 Cr. App. R. 219, 221 (C.C.A.).

73. R. v. Cohen (1909) 2 Cr. App. R. 196, 208 (C.C.A.) (Channell, J.). See also R. v. Mason (1924) 18 Cr. App. R. 131 (C.C.A.); Clouston v. Corry, [1906] A.C. 122, 130 (P.C.).

74. R. v. Tillman, *The Guardian,* Feb. 6, 1962 (C.C.A.). See also R. v. Dinnick (1909) 3 Cr. App. R. 77 (C.C.A.); R. v. Mills (1935) 25 Cr. App. R. 138 (C.C.A.).

75. R. v. Canny (1945) 30 Cr. App. R. 143 (C.C.A.).

jury, not the judge, to decide on the weight of the defense, no matter how absurd it may seem to be or how unlikely it is that any sensible person would give it the least attention. In fact, the prisoner is entitled to hope that it may be his great good fortune to find a stupid jury that will believe his story. While a conviction will not be quashed, where a miscarriage of justice did not occur,[76] even though the judge made strong or even immoderate remarks in his summing-up, the judge must leave it absolutely to the jury to make up their minds about the evidence, and he has no license to make a prosecution speech.[77] In any event, the rules clearly give the judge a great deal of discretion in fashioning his summing-up, and it has been observed that "an experienced judge can so marshall the facts and indicate the probabilities that, while professing to leave everything to the jury, he has in truth made their verdict himself. A tendentious summing-up becomes all the more persuasive when it is not dogmatic and purports to leave an unfettered choice to the jury." [78]

It remains to be noted that the English judge is free to comment on the failure of the accused to testify.[79] Since 1898 the law of England has permitted an accused person to give evidence at any stage of the proceedings,[80] and he is privileged to make an unsworn statement in court, thus avoiding cross-examination. The statute also provides that he cannot be compelled

76. R. v. Hepworth (1910) 4 Cr. App. R. 128 (C.C.A.).

77. R. v. Blackley, [1963] Crim. L. Rev. 443 (C.C.A.).

78. Williams, *The Proof of Guilt*, p. 287.

79. In 1965, the U.S. Supreme Court ruled that due process forbids comment by state judges, thus applying to all the states the previous federal rule against comment. Griffin v. California, 380 U.S. 609 (1965).

80. Criminal Evidence Act, 1898, s. 1. See R. K. Berg, "Criminal Procedure: France, England, and the United States," 8 DePaul L. Rev. 256–348, esp. 264–76, 302–30 (1959).

to give evidence,[81] and that the prosecution may not comment on the silence of the accused.[82] The statute did not say, however, that the judge may not comment, and the following year it was held that in his discretion, if he thinks it proper, the judge may comment on the defendant's failure to testify.[83] "The nature and degree of such comment," the court said, "must rest entirely in the discretion of the judge who tries the case." The Lord Chief Justice, Lord Goddard, has observed that there is nothing unfair in the judge's commenting on the silence of the accused because "nowadays, . . . everybody knows that absence from the witness box requires a great deal of explanation. . . ." [84] In very recent decisions, while approving of comment, the Court of Criminal Appeal has called attention to the desirability of the judge's reminding the jury that the failure of the accused to give evidence should not be held

81. *Ibid.*, s. 1 (a). Of course, the accused may waive his privilege against self-incrimination by choosing to testify, and if he does so he is punishable for perjury. R. v. Wookey (1899) 63 J.P. 409 (Worcester Assizes). Having decided to testify, he is subject to cross-examination and may not refuse to answer questions because the answers will incriminate him. If he refuses to answer on such grounds, he is punishable for contempt. R. v. Senior (1899) 34 L.J. 100 (C.C.C.); R. v. Minihane (1921) 16 Cr. App. R. 38 (C.C.A.).

82. *Ibid.*, s. 1 (b): "The failure of any person charged with an offence, or of the wife or husband, as the case may be, of the person so charged, to give evidence shall not be made the subject of any comment by the prosecution."

83. R. v. Rhodes, [1899] 1 Q.B. 77 (C.C.R.). See also Kops v. R., [1894] A.C. 650, 653 (P.C.); R. v. Bernard, (1908) 1 Cr. App. R. 218, 219 (C.C.A.). It is improper, however, for the judge to comment on the failure of the defendant to give explanation to the police. R. v. Naylor (1932) 23 Cr. App. R. 177 (C.C.A.); R. v. Leckey, [1944] 1 K.B. 80, 86 (C.C.A.). See Williams, *The Proof of Guilt*, pp. 57–63.

84. R. v. Jackson, [1953] 1 W.L.R. 591, 594 (C.C.A.). See also R. v. Smith (1915) 84 L.J.K.B. 2153, 11 Cr. App. R. 229 (C.C.A.); R. v. Voisin, [1918] 1 K.B. 531 (C.C.A.).

against him,[85] and has stressed that the judge must not suggest that the defendant's failure to testify was inconsistent with innocence or that the only reasonable inference is one of guilt.[86] Even so, a judge may go too far. The Privy Council quashed a conviction in 1950 because the judge made excessive comment on the defendant's failure to give evidence: he had drawn attention to this fact nine times.[87] Lord Oaksey observed that "the very fact that the prosecution are not permitted to comment on that fact shows how careful a judge should be in making such comment. . . . The judge's repeated comments . . . may well have led the jury to think that no innocent man could have taken such a course." [88]

85. R. v. Baines, [1963] Crim. L. Rev. 210 (C.C.A.).

86. R. v. Fisher, [1964] Crim. L. Rev. 150 (C.C.A.). In 1965 the U.S. Supreme Court ruled that it was violative of due process for a state trial judge to instruct the jury that the silence of the defendant as to evidence of which he had knowledge could be considered as evidence of guilt. Griffin v. California, 380 U.S. 609 (1965).

87. Waugh v. R., [1950] A.C. 203 (P.C.).

88. *Id.* at 211, 212.

VI

An Evaluation

It is a fundamental fact of English life that the law courts of the country are widely trusted and admired. Understandably, this view is shared by the judges themselves and by political leaders. There is an old aphorism in Britain that "if justice had a voice, she would speak like an English judge."[1] Thus, Lord Cockburn, the Lord Chief Justice, observed in an opinion rendered in 1861, "I have been some years at the bar and on the bench, and have seen much of the administration of justice; and I never saw a Judge, from rashness, vanity, or impatience, lend himself to oppression, or do anything not right, to his knowledge and belief, between the Crown and the party accused."[2] Or as an earlier chief justice, Lord Ellenborough, remarked in 1804, "the law of England is a law of liberty."[3] Speaking in the House of Commons in 1954, Sir Winston Churchill

1. Quoted by Sir Alfred Denning, *The Road to Justice* (London: Stevens, 1955), p. 10.
2. R. v. Charlesworth (1861) 1 B. & S. 460, 505, 121 E.R. 786, 803 (K.B.).
3. R. v. Cobbett (1804) 29 St. Tr. 1, 49.

said, "The British Judiciary, with its traditions and record, is one of the greatest living assets of our race and people and the independence of the Judiciary is a part of our message to the ever-growing world which is rising so swiftly around us." [4] Lord Hewart, another chief justice, expressed a similar sentiment when he remarked, at the Lord Mayor's banquet in 1936, that "His Majesty's Judges are satisfied with the *almost* universal admiration in which they are held." [5] Even greater smugness was expressed by the Solicitor-General, Sir Peter Rawlinson, in a more recent speech to the Cambridge University Conservative Association, when he asserted that the English legal system was the most widely admired in the world, and went on to say, "There is no substantial evidence to support the idea of legal reform in this country at the present time." [6]

Actually, there is some reason for agreement with the views of an English solicitor who remarked in a book published in 1932 that "it is unfortunately a fact that this country is singularly uncritical of itself and its institutions," and who went on to say that "the theory of the perfection of English Justice is humbug." [7] Competent scholars have recently noted that attacks on the criminal law and procedure have been increasing,[8] and the excellent *Criminal Law Review* declared editorially in 1963 that "calls for the reform of the law and of the

4. 538 H.C. Deb., Hansard, March 23, 1954, col. 1063.
5. *The Times*, Nov. 10, 1936, p. 21.
6. *The Times*, Oct. 28, 1963, p. 12.
7. "Solicitor," *English Justice* (London: Routledge, 1932), p. ix.
8. See Gerald Gardiner and Andrew Martin, eds., *Law Reform Now* (London: Victor Gollancz, 1963); J. C. Wood, "General Principles of the Criminal Law," [1964] Crim. L. Rev. 9–22; D. S. Davies, "The House of Lords and the Criminal Law" (1961) 6 J. Soc. Pub. Teach. Law 104.

legal system are these days many and vociferous." [9]
There is, among other things, the hard fact that there
is a great deal of crime in England. It is a "disquieting
feature of our society," a White Paper on penal policy
recently remarked, "that . . . rising standards in material prosperity, education and social welfare have
brought no decrease in the high rate of crime reached
during the war." [10]

English criminal law has been criticized by competent
authorities for its "rambling formlessness," and it has
been emphasized that systematic review is today badly
needed.[11] The lack of scholarly interest in the law
touching on civil liberties was noted by a distinguished
professor of public law at the University of London in
his inaugural address in 1960.[12] There has always been
a great deal of criticism of the accusatorial nature of an
English criminal trial,[13] and favorable attention has
often been called to the French system of justice, which
puts the investigative and preparatory function in the
hands of a judge (*juge d'instruction*) rather than in the
hands of the police, as in Britain.[14]

9. [1963] Crim. L. Rev. 667.

10. White Paper on Penal Policy, *Penal Practice in a Changing
Society*, 1959, Cmd. 645, quoted by Barbara Wootton in *Crime and the
Criminal Law* (London: Stevens, 1963), p. 31.

11. D. R. S. Davies, Professor of Law at the University of Liverpool,
"Reform of the Criminal Law," in *Law Reform and Law Making*
(Cambridge: W. Heffer, 1953), pp. 65–73, 66.

12. S. A. deSmith, *The Lawyers and the Constitution* (London:
G. Bell, 1960), p. 14: "It is remarkable how little work has been
done on the legal aspects of civil liberty in England during this
century, especially since 1945."

13. See, e.g., Louis Blom-Cooper, *The A6 Murder: Regina v. James
Hanratty* (London: Penguin Books, 1963), p. 132: "The English
criminal process is concerned not with the truth about the crime, but
solely with the assessment of criminal responsibility."

14. See Morris Ploscowe, "The Development of Present-Day Criminal Procedures in Europe and America," 48 Harv. L. Rev. 433–73

An American observer is always impressed by the lofty status of the judge in English society. A judge of the Supreme Court or of the House of Lords is truly a great man of the realm, and clearly he is master of the courtroom. Lawyers speak deferentially and respectfully to him, and no English judge would permit lawyers to bully witnesses or take unfair advantage of a situation.[15] James Bradley Thayer once observed that "it must be remembered that in England the judges have always, in theory, been great ministers of the Crown; and that even to this day much of the reality and many visible signs and symbols of this high place and power remain."[16] Lord Evershed recently reminded us that English judges are members of an "independent, learned profession," and that they have not in recent times been involved in matters of political controversy.[17] The status of the English judge is reflected in the physical atmosphere of the courtroom. Englishmen as well as Americans are impressed by the robes and wigs, by the orderliness and dignified progress of the trial, by the

(1935); Robert Vonin, "The Protection of the Accused in French Criminal Procedure," 5 Int'l. and Comp. L. Q. 1, 25 (1956); Robert Vonin, "L'Affaire Drummond," [1955] Crim. L. Rev. 5–12; Edwin R. Keedy, "The Preliminary Investigation of Crime in France," 88 U. Pa. L. Rev. 385–424, 692–727, 915–33 (1940). Professor Vonin, who teaches law at the University of Bordeaux, points out that there can be no trial unless "grave presumptions of guilt" are first established, and that in France this is a judicial and not a police function. French law forbids police interrogation, and if the accused has elected to be assisted by counsel, then there can be no questioning by the magistrate except in the presence of counsel. Evidence secured in violation of law must be excluded. 5 Int'l. and Comp. L. Q. 16 (1956).

15. See Glanville Williams, *The Proof of Guilt* (2nd ed.; London: Stevens, 1958), Chap. 2.

16. James Bradley Thayer, *A Preliminary Treatise on Evidence at the Common Law* (Boston: Little, Brown, 1898), p. 207.

17. Lord Evershed, "The Judicial Process in Twentieth Century England," 61 Colum. L. Rev. 761–91, 763, 773 (1961).

respectfulness of counsel toward the bench, and by the crisp promptness of those who sit on the bench. Some time ago a competent American observer remarked that "the conduct of English trials—both those taking place in courts of summary jurisdiction and before juries—is distinguished by order, dignity, urbanity and dispatch."[18]

Even of this aspect of English justice, however, one finds rather trenchant criticism. In a recent lecture Barbara Wootton described the atmosphere of the higher courts as "an atmosphere of archaic majesty and ritual. Moreover, the members of the Bar,[19] whether on or off the Bench, constitute a sodality that is, surely, unique among English professions; nor is there anything in their training which might widen their social horizons or enlarge their social observations. In consequence, there is perhaps no place in English life where the divisions of our society are more obtrusive: nowhere where one is more conscious of the division into 'them'

18. Pendleton Howard, *Criminal Justice in England* (New York: Macmillan, 1931), p. 403.

19. By the Bar Miss Wootton meant the barristers, who alone have the right of audience in the higher courts. There are only about two thousand barristers in the whole country, tightly organized in the four Inns of Court which are controlled by little groups known as "Benchers." Almost all judges of the higher courts are drawn from this small circle. Furthermore, barristers do not deal directly with clients, but only with solicitors, and thus their contacts with the judges are far closer than their contacts with clients. For a lively account of the English Bar see Henry Cecil, *Brief to Counsel* (London: Michael Joseph, 1958). Cf. the remarks of Sir Patrick Devlin, *The Criminal Prosecution in England* (New Haven: Yale University Press, 1958), p. 26: "A judge is always appointed from the Bar; he will have worked with and against many senior men who appear before him and he continually meets them in the Inns of Court and at the Bar messes while on circuit. This makes for community of thought between Bench and Bar. In this sort of atmosphere the spirit of the law is often more important than the letter. . . ."

and 'us.' " [20] Similarly, J. B. Priestly recently wrote, "I cannot help feeling suspicious about all this majesty business, the dressing up and parading, the theatrical effects. Why does the Law have to look and behave as if it wanted to suggest that Judge Jeffreys and the Bloody Assize are only just around the corner, or as if some final document, heavy and stiff with sealing wax, will have to be signed by Queen Anne? Why is it at all times trying to overawe us, to stun us into dazed submission? Why does it not recognize that we are the citizens who foot the bill, not rebellious but defeated peasants now facing an army of occupation? If something genuinely practical, sensible, reasonable, helpful, is about to be attempted, then why go to the trouble and expense of all this theatrical production, creating an atmosphere in which it looks as if the practical, the sensible, the reasonable, the helpful, will never be given a chance?" And finally, said Mr. Priestly, "although there are a few liberal-minded wig-and-robe men, water carriers in the desert, this wiggery and robery represents a leathery, tough binding of conservatism defying any reformer, any radical, indeed any man who believes that England will soon have to save herself, body and soul." [21]

It has also been observed that the rather awesome majesty of the high courts of the realm does not exist in some of the police courts of the cities. While many of the magistrates' courts over which stipendiary magistrates preside are very good, in some, the Conservative Bow Group recently declared, "both lay men and women are bullied and chivied and treated in a way which

20. Barbara Wootton, *Crime and the Criminal Law*, p. 32.
21. "Wigs and Robes," New Statesman, LXIV (August 17, 1962), 196–97.

sometimes ignores even the most elementary rules of civilised behaviour; the sentencing of offenders tends to be haphazard and sometimes almost savage. Fortunately such courts are rare. . . ." [22]

The use of the lay, untrained justice of the peace is a familiar cause of concern in England. According to the famous Bow Group of reform-minded Conservatives, the justices lack legal training and knowledge, and rely too much on their clerks. In their report published in 1962, the Bow Group drew attention to some of the defects of the magistrates' courts. At times, they said, there is "the almost total disregard . . . for the burden of proof properly placed on the prosecution by our law," which means that magistrates tend to accept the policeman's word uncritically.[23] Indeed, they said, "the magistrates' courts system as it exists throughout most of the country is a splendid example of the English delight in amateurism." [24]

A Royal Commission, reporting in 1948, recommended that "what we think is possible and should be done is to train justices to understand the nature of

22. Bow Group Pamphlet, *Scales of Justice* (London: Conservative Political Center, 1962), p. 10.

23. *Scales of Justice,* p. 13. For a blistering attack on the magistrates' courts, see "Solicitor," *English Justice,* Chap. 2. Here the charge was made that party service was a principal qualification for the appointment of justices, and that many were too old, were lacking in judicial qualities, and were strongly prejudiced. It was claimed that those who plead guilty are treated more generously, that the justices abused their power of cross-examination, and that the clerk had too much power without responsibility. "The unpaid magistrates," the writer concluded, "constitute the worst feature of English Justice" (*ibid.,* p. 247).

24. *Scales of Justice,* p. 9. Since the magistrates' court is mainly a criminal court, the Bow Group would take away from it any civil jurisdiction, as, for example, in cases of civil debts, and in matrimonial and bastardy cases (*ibid.,* p. 15).

their own duties rather than the substantive law that they administer."[25] The commission thought that it would be desirable for the justice to comprehend the nature of "a submission that there is no case to answer," that he should know "at least enough" about the law of evidence "to enable him to avoid mistakes in any questions that he may ask," and that he should understand the various courses of action open to him in deciding what to do with an offender.[26] Nevertheless, on the whole the commission commended the system of lay justices, "because, like that of trial by jury, it gives the citizen a part to play in the administration of the law. It emphasizes the fact that the principles of the common law, and even the language of statutes, ought to be (as in the case of the common law at least, they certainly are) comprehensible by any intelligent person without specialized training. Its continuance prevents the growth of a suspicion in the ordinary man's mind that the law is a mystery which must be left to a professional caste and has little in common with justice as the layman understands it. Further, the cases in which decisions on questions of fact in criminal cases are left to one man ought to be, as they now are, exceptional. It must be remembered that even a judge of the High Court is never asked to undertake the heavy responsibility of trying a criminal case except with the assistance of a jury of laymen, to whom alone is left the decision on the facts."[27]

The expensiveness of English justice has often been commented on, though the extensive system of legal

25. Report of the Royal Commission on Justices of the Peace, 1948, Cmd. 7463, p. 23.
26. *Ibid.*
27. *Ibid.*, p. 55.

aid in civil as well as criminal actions has done much to reduce the burden of litigation on the poor. Even so, as the undersecretary of The Law Society, Mr. E. J. T. Mathews, pointed out in a recent address to the British Academy of Forensic Sciences, it is difficult for an indigent defendant to enjoy the assistance of scientific experts, and since the prosecution has available the great resources of the Home Office Forensic Science Laboratories, it follows that "the scales are tilted in favor of the prosecution." [28] It is true that the Home Office issued a circular (No. 158) in 1957 directing that "the result of any examination made by the Home Office Forensic Science Laboratory which might have any bearing on the case should be communicated to the defendant or his legal representative whether or not it is proposed to call a member of the staff of the laboratory as a witness," but Mr. Mathews made the point that in some parts of the country this is not done.[29]

Another familiar complaint about English justice involves the factor of delay. A Home Office study of a 1956 sample indicated that for all courts, the average time between committal by the magistrates and trial was thirty-six days.[30] For courts that are in continuous session, such as the Central Criminal Court, the time lapse was twenty-nine days, and in large Assize districts where the court sits three or four times a year, the average was fifty-four days. For persons on bail, the average time was forty days, and for persons in custody, thirty-one days. Thus the study indicated that the interval was shorter where courts sit continuously or nearly so, where persons are in custody instead of being

28. Quoted in *Scales of Justice,* p. 32.
29. *Ibid.,* p. 33.
30. Evelyn Gibson, *Time Spent Awaiting Trial,* Home Office Research Unit Report (London: H.M.S.O., 1960).

out on bail, and where the plea is guilty rather than not guilty. The average time between sentencing and the disposition of a criminal appeal is rarely more than a month.[31]

An interdepartmental committee, the Streatfeild Committee, published a report in February, 1961, in which delay was the major theme.[32] Its findings indicated that in 1957, five thousand defendants waited eight weeks or more for trial, twelve hundred waited twelve weeks or more, and four hundred waited sixteen weeks.[33] The committee complained of the lack of good statistics on this subject. "Everyone is agreed," it wrote, "that an accused person should be quickly brought to trial, but few of our witnesses felt able to give a definite opinion on whether under our system trials in fact take place within a reasonable time." [34] The committee called attention to the objections to delay: [35]

1. . . . the benefits which flow from justice being done will be more potent if it is done quickly. Where a crime has caused concern and anxiety, whether nationally or locally, it is in the public interest that there would be no avoidable delay. . . .
2. . . . if there is long delay, there is a risk that the evidence may be stale and that in consequence justice may not be done. Witnesses' recollections are not as fresh months after the event and some important detail may be forgotten.

31. Delmar Karlen, *Appellate Courts in the United States and England* (New York: New York University Press, 1963), p. 115.
32. Report of the Interdepartmental Committee on the Business of the Criminal Courts, 1961, Cmd. 1289.
33. *Ibid.*, p. 3.
34. The computation indicated that while the interval between committal and trial was about five weeks, on the average, as indicated in the 1960 Home Office study, the total actual waiting time varied from two weeks to four months.
35. *Ibid.*, p. 6, paras. 15, 16, 17, 18.

3. . . . some witnesses, especially the victims of assaults, view with apprehension the prospect of describing an unpleasant incident in formal evidence for the second time. If this period of apprehension is protracted, it can cause real distress and in the case of children can have undesirable side-effects.
4. . . . the interval is an anxious period for the accused himself.

While the Streatfeild Committee recognized that the English figures were better than those of other countries—and they are certainly better than comparable American figures—it felt that even so there was no ground for complacency, in view of the fact that in about a fourth of all the cases the waiting period was longer than eight weeks. Its report led to the adoption of the Criminal Justice Administration Act, 1962, the objective of which is to reduce the waiting period to no more than eight weeks, except in the most exceptional cases.[36]

The Court of Criminal Appeal has from its inception in 1907 been the subject of a great deal of discussion in England. Its inability to order a new trial was always a bone of contention, though this has at long last been remedied with the adoption of the Criminal Appeal Act, 1964. Its lack of an official shorthand report of its work has often been noted. In 1927 the Lord Chief Justice, Lord Hewart, "referred to the grave inconvenience to the Court that there was not an official shorthand report of appeals," and he expressed the hope that some day such a report would be available.[37] But this has not yet come about. An English legal scholar recently observed, "This is the 20th century. It is a

36. See Alec Samuels, "The Criminal Justice Administration Act, 1962," [1962] Crim. L. Rev. 285–99.
37. R. v. Walters (1927) 20 Cr. App. R. 69 (C.C.A.).

pitiable spectacle to see a final Court of Appeal dependent for a record of its own judgments on the providence of the transcripts of shorthand notes taken on behalf of odd Clerks of the Peace or of the shorter notes taken by private publishers." [38] But most significant of all, it is often pointed out that the Court of Criminal Appeal is not a true appellate court, since the judges of this court are also trial judges. Thus the Queen's Bench judges who sit on this court often review the decisions made previously by other Queen's Bench judges, of the very same rank, in their capacity as Assize court judges. Accordingly, it has been suggested that the Court of Criminal Appeal should be detached altogether from the Queen's Bench and made a division of the Court of Appeal, which is at the present time a separate appellate branch of the Supreme Court of Judicature for civil cases. [39]

While it cannot be said that the English system of justice is perfect (as indeed no system is), and while further reform is necessary and is being urged in responsible circles of British life, there is worldwide admiration for a system which displays such solicitude for the plight of one who is accused of crime. For one thing, the English system depends on a great deal of collaboration on the part of unpaid lay magistrates and unofficial persons, such as jurors and private prosecu-

38. D. Seaborne Davies, "The Court of Criminal Appeal: The First Forty Years," 1 J. Soc. Pub. Teach. Law 425–41, 426 (1951).

39. See Gerald Gardiner and F. F. Jones, "The Administration of Justice," in *Law Reform Now*, Gardiner and Martin, eds., p. 17. This was the principal recommendation of the Donovan Committee, which reported in August, 1965. It proposed that the functions of the present Court of Criminal Appeal be transferred to a new division of the Court of Appeal, to be called the Criminal Division of that Court. Report of the Interdepartmental Committee on the Court of Criminal Appeal, 1965, Cmd. 2755, para. 320.

tors.[40] Thus the system remains in some measure responsive to the people, though it cannot be denied that a rather small, professional caste wields enormous power. Furthermore, a genuine effort has been made to give the accused, the weaker party, a measure of equality with the representatives of government on the other side, not only through a comprehensive system of legal aid, but also by the operation of rules of evidence and procedure. The presumption, for example, is always one of innocence, and the heavy burden of proving guilt beyond reasonable doubt rests on the Crown. The powers of arrest and detention pending trial are strictly limited.[41] The prosecution is duty-bound to place fairly before the court all relevant evidence, and its *raison d'être* is not to get convictions but rather to serve the ends of justice.[42] The judges are given a large discretion in the management of trials and in the determination of penalties. Trials must be public, and judges may in-

40. Sir Theobald Mathew, a former Director of Public Prosecutions, has written: "The lesson to be learned from a study of the history of the criminal law is that we have secured and preserved our individual liberty and security by evolving a system under which these still depend ultimately not upon an executive, however benevolent, nor upon a judiciary, however wise, but upon the active support and the final judgment of our fellow citizens." *The Office and Duties of the Director of Public Prosecutions* (London: University of London Press, 1950), p. 16.

41. The Council of the Law Society made a survey of police practices in 1962 and concluded that police forces in Britain "perform their various duties in a competent and efficient manner, and maintain a high standard of integrity." But it was clear from the Council's findings that there is some variation in the manner in which the police carry out their duties in different areas. The Council also expressed the opinion that generally speaking the Judges' Rules were fair and provided adequate safeguards, and that their great defect was that they lack clear legal status. Margaret Puxon, "The Law Society and the Police" (1963) 107 S.J. 881–82.

42. See Denning, *The Road to Justice*, pp. 41–42.

voke principles of natural justice in the effort to see that the right thing is done. Most impressive to an American observer are the strict limitations which English law imposes on the police in regard to interrogation. While evidence secured unlawfully is admissible, if relevant, the English rules on the admissibility of confessions are strict enough to satisfy the most sensitive taste.

A news story that appeared in the *Daily Telegraph* on September 19, 1961, should convince anyone that, in the area of criminal justice, British taste is fastidious indeed.

TRIAL BY JURY
NOT POLICE
SAYS JUDGE

Daily Telegraph Reporter

Two Plymouth CID men were called into the witness box by Mr. Justice STREATFEILD at Hampshire Assizes yesterday and accused of trying to break down a man by interrogation.

"I will consider whether I do not report it to the Chief Constable of Plymouth," said the Judge. "I hope that is not the common practice in Plymouth."

Det. Insp. WILLIAMS and Det. Con. WICKSTEED were rebuked after the Judge directed the jury to return a verdict of not guilty against DAVID POWELL HANNAH, 38, of Fountain Crescent, Plymouth. Hannah, married with two children, pleaded not guilty to having unlawful sexual intercourse with a teenage girl.

"CANNOT TELL LIES"

When called to give evidence, the girl broke down in the witness box and sobbed: "I cannot tell lies, even though I hate him so much."

When called to the witness box Det. Con. WICKSTEED agreed that after Hannah denied the girl's allegations, he had asked Hannah why she should have invented such a story. He also told Hannah he believed her.

THE JUDGE: "Do you appreciate that in this country we have trial by jury, and not by police officers? What business has a police officer to tell a person who is being interrogated that the police are convinced that the girl is not telling lies? It is done intending to try and break him down, is it not?"

Det. Con. WICKSTEED: "As far as I am concerned. I was letting him know exactly what I did think. I can only apologise."

Index

Index

Administration of Justice Act, 1960, 13, 65

Administration of Justice Act, 1964, 7

Alverstone, Lord Chief Justice: on police interrogation, 35

Appeal: to Quarter Sessions, 8; to the High Court, 8; to a divisional court, 9; to the Court of Criminal Appeal, 9–13; to the House of Lords, 13

Arrest: law of, 14–22; private, 15–16; by police officers, 16–19; without warrant, 17–18; resistance to unlawful, 20

Ashworth, J.: on arrest, 15; on the burden of proof, 108

Assize, Courts of: defined, 6–7; barring public from, 73; and appeals, 84; judges in, 127; mentioned passim

Atkin, Lord: on arrest, 19; on the burden of proof, 105

Atkinson, J.: on bail, 26; on public trial, 72

Attorney-General: on appeals, 13, and nolle prosequi, 28, 31; and consent to prosecute, 29, 31; and Director of Public Prosecutions, 30

Bail: law of, 20–28; granting of, 20–21; to whom available, 21–23; and bailsmen, 24–25; excessive, 25–26; reform of, 27–28

Barry, J.: on the law of arrest, 14

Bentham: on public trial, 71

Betting Act, 1853, 94

Bill of Rights, 1688, 25

Blackburn, Lord: on invasion of private rights, 4

Blackstone: on trial by jury, 97

Board of Trade: prosecutions by, 29

Bow Group, 121, 122

Burden of proof, 5, 103–10; and presumption of innocence, 104–5, 106, 107; and behavior of judges, 106–10

Bushell's Case, 100

Butler, R. A.: on police interrogation, 35

Camden, Lord: on general search warrants, 53; on trial by jury, 97

Campbell, Lord: on arrest, 16–17

"Case stated" procedure, 8–10

Cassels, J.: on the independence of the jury, 101

Central Criminal Court (Old Bailey), 7–8, 9, 84, 87, 124

Children and Young Persons Act, 1933, 55, 74

Churchill, Sir Winston: on the British judiciary, 116–17

City of London: Common Serjeant, 8; Recorder, 8

133

City of London Court, 8
Clerks of the Peace, 127
Cockburn, Lord Chief Justice: on English judges, 116
Coinage Offences Act, 1936, 16, 29, 55
Coke, Lord: on the right to counsel, 81
Coleridge, J.: on double jeopardy, 91
Common Pleas, Court of, 64
Confessions: law of, 45–52, 59–60
Cook, Peter, 101–2
Counsel: right to, 80–88; fees of, 86–87
Court of Appeal, 66
Court of Criminal Appeal: make-up of, 9; appeal to, 9–10, 12–13; power to order new trial, 11–13; appeal to House of Lords, 13; on arrest, 20; on bail, 23, 26; on the Judges' Rules, 37; on confessions, 47; on the necessity of evidence, 69; on trial of uncounseled defendants, 81; on double jeopardy, 94–95; on trial by jury, 98, 100, 101, 103; on the burden of proof, 106–9; on comment by the judge, 111–12, 114; criticisms of, 126–27
Criminal Appeal Act, 1907, 9, 10, 107
Criminal Appeal Act, 1964, 12–13, 126–27
Criminal Cases Act, 1908: costs in, 22
Criminal Justice Administration Act, 1962, 126
Criminal Law Review, 44, 117
Criminal Law Revision Committee, 99
Criminal Libel Act, 1819, 55
Criminal Procedure Act, 1851, 89

Crown Courts, 8, 9, 84
Crown Courts Act, 1956, 8
Customs and Excise Act, 1952, 30

Daily Telegraph, 129
Dangerous Drugs Act, 1951, 29
Darling, Justice: on the right to a public trial, 74
Denning, Lord: on arrest, 14–15; on prosecution counsel, 33; on basic principles of justice, 67
De Smith, S. A., 118
Devlin, Lord: on prosecution counsel, 33; on the jury system, 98
Dicey, A. V.: on habeas corpus, 61
Director of Public Prosecutions, 28–33 *passim*
Dock brief, 87–88. *See also* Counsel
Double jeopardy: law of, 88–96

Edward III, 5
Elias v. *Pasmore,* 57
Ellenborough, Lord Chief Justice: on English law, 116
Entick v. *Carrington,* 53
Evershed, Lord: on English judges, 119
Evidence wrongfully secured: use of, 46, 59–61; admissibility of, 58–59. *See also* Searches and seizures
Exchequer, Court of, 64
Exclusionary rule, 57–58. *See also* Searches and seizures

Fair trial: elements of, 67–68; and right of accused to be present, 68; and right to notice, 68; and right of cross-examination, 69; and right to impartial judge, 70; and freedom from newspaper comment, 70–71

Forgery Act, 1913, 54
Frankfurter, Justice: on police interrogation, 34; on the Judges' Rules, 36

General Council of the Bar, 88
Goddard, Lord Chief Justice: on bail, 22–23; on admissibility of evidence secured unlawfully, 58–59; on habeas corpus, 63; on concept of natural justice, 78–80; on jury trial, 102; on the burden of proof, 108; on comment by the judge, 114
Goodhart, A. L.: on concept of natural justice, 75

Habeas corpus, writ of, 4, 61–66
Habeas Corpus Acts, 61
Haldane, Lord: on public trials, 73
Hallam, Henry: on habeas corpus, 61
Halsbury, Lord: on habeas corpus, 61
Hardwicke, Lord: on reporting of trials by newspapers, 70
Herschell, Lord: on fair trial, 68
Hewart, Lord Chief Justice: on fair trial, 67; on justices' clerks, 70; on the burden of proof, 103; on English judges, 117; on the Court of Criminal Appeal, 126
High Commission Court, 52
High Court of Justice, 7, 8, 9, 14, 17, 22, 25, 35, 51, 57, 64, 70, 72, 73, 93, 123. See also Assize, Courts of
Hodson, Lord: on concept of natural justice, 77
Home Office: study on bail, 26–27; and appointment of the Director of Public Prosecutions,

30; on police interrogation, 35; on the Judges' Rules, 43; and the Forensic Science Laboratories, 124; and study of delay of courts, 124–25
Home Secretary: and clemency, 12; and arrest, 18–19; on prosecutions, 29; on the Judges' Rules, 35; and wiretapping, 58; on counsel fees, 86
House of Lords: appeals to, 13; on the law of arrest, 18–19; on habeas corpus, 63, 65–66; on public trial, 72–73; on concept of natural justice, 75–76; on double jeopardy, 94–95; on the burden of proof, 107; on inadmissible evidence, 111
Humphreys, J.: on double jeopardy, 92

Indictable Offences Act, 1848, 82
Innocence, presumption of. See Burden of proof
Interpretation Act, 1889, 89
Irish Rebellion, 74

Judges' Rules, 34–45, 48
Jury: trial by, 4, 97–103; challenging of, 99–100; impartiality of, 100; independence of, 100–2; unanimous vote of, 102–3. See also Fair trial; Trial
Justice, 44
Justice, English form of: and protection of individuals, 3–5; and burden of proof, 5, 103–11; and the specific courts, 5–8; and the right to appeal, 38–43; and the right to a fair trial, 67–71; and concept of natural justice, 75–80; and law of comment by judges, 111–15; and prestige of judiciary, 116–20;

Justice (*continued*)
criticisms of, 120–29; and need
for reform, 122–29
Justices of the peace, 5–6, 18,
122–23

King's Bench Court, 64

Larceny Act, 1916, 16
Law of Libel Amendment Act,
1888, 30
Lawrence, A. T.: on voluntary
statements by prisoners, 36
Law Society, 86, 87, 124
Legal aid: for the poor, 83–88;
certificates, 84–85; area com-
mittees, 85–86. *See also* Counsel
Legal Aid and Advice Act, 1949,
83
Licensing Act, 1910, 94
London, Metropolitan, courts of,
7–8

MacDermott, Lord Chief Justice:
on criminal trials, 4
Magistrates, stipendiary, 5, 7
Magistrates' courts, 5, 121–23 and
passim
Magistrates' Courts Act, 1952, 83
Malicious Damage Act, 1861, 16
Mathew, Sir Theobald: on the
Director of Public Prosecutions,
32
Mathews, E. J. T.: on the de-
fense of indigents, 124
Maugham, Lord: on arrest, 18;
on the right to counsel, 82
Ministry of Labor: prosecutions
by, 29

Newspapers: reporting of trials
by, 70–71
North Briton, 53

Oaksey, Lord: on comment, 115
Obscene Publications Acts, 1857,
1959: 55
Offences against the Person Act,
1861, 18
Official Secrets Acts, 1911, 1920:
55, 74

Parker, Lord Chief Justice: on
the taking of new evidence by
the Court of Criminal Appeal,
10; on police interrogation, 43;
on habeas corpus, 64; on concept of natural justice, 78–79
Petty Sessions courts, 7, 8, 72
Police: arrests, 16–19; and attitude toward bail, 25, 26–27;
interrogation, law of, 34–45;
and confessions, 46, 47, 48, 49,
50; and searching of prisoners,
56; and searching of premises,
56–57
Poor Prisoner's Defence Acts,
1903, 1930: 83
Post Office Act, 1953, 30
Post Office Department: prosecutions by, 29, 30
Priestly, J. B.: on English courts,
121
Privy Council: on the admissibility of evidence, 59; on comment by judges, 115
Prosecution: law of, 28–33; private, 28–29; by departments,
29, 30; statutory control of,
29–30; by the Director of Public Prosecutions, 31–33
Public Order Act, 1936, 29

Quarter Sessions, courts of: defined, 6; powers of, 8; and bail,
22; appeals to, 84; Clerk of the
Peace in, 87; and *passim*
Queen's Bench Division, 6–7, 8,

9, 13, 18, 21, 35, 64, 77, 79, 127

R. v. *Connelly,* 94–95
Rawlinson, Sir Peter: on English justice, 117
Reading, Lord: on public trial, 74; on comment, 111
Reid, Lord: on concept of natural justice, 77
Royal Commission on the Police, 1960, 14

Sankey, Lord: on the burden of proof, 107
Searches and seizures: law of, 52–59; and search warrants, 52–57 *passim;* and search of persons, 56, 57; and interceptions, 58–59; and wiretapping, 58
Simon, Viscount: on arrest without warrant, 19
Simonds, Lord: on arrest, 19–20
Smith, J. C.: on the Judges' Rules, 44
Star Chamber, 52
Streatfeild Committee: on delay in court cases, 125–26
Sumner, Lord: on coerced confessions, 49–50

Tenterden, Lord: on the right to counsel, 83
Thayer, James Bradley: on English judges, 119
Trespass, action of: 4
Trial: order for new, 11–13, 126–27; right to, by accused, 71–75; and concept of natural justice, 77–79; and right to counsel, 81–88; and double jeopardy, 88–96 *passim;* and summing up by judges, 111–13; delay of, 124–26. *See also* Fair trial; Jury

Warrants: arrest without, 17–18, 19; general, 52–53
Wilkes, John, 53
Williams, Glanville: on the jury system, 98
Wiretapping, 58
Wootton, Barbara: on English justice, 120